ALSO BY ALEXIS OKEOWO

A Moonless, Starless Sky:
Ordinary Women and Men Fighting Extremism in Africa

BLESSINGS
AND
DISASTERS

BLESSINGS AND DISASTERS

a story of Alabama

Alexis Okeowo

HENRY HOLT AND COMPANY
NEW YORK

Henry Holt and Company
Publishers since 1866
120 Broadway
New York, New York 10271
www.henryholt.com

Henry Holt® and 𝐇® are registered trademarks of Macmillan
Publishing Group, LLC.

Library of Congress Cataloging-in-Publication Data

Names: Okeowo, Alexis, author.
Title: Blessings and disasters : a story of Alabama / Alexis Okeowo.
Description: First edition. | New York : Henry Holt and Company,
2025. | Includes bibliographical references.
Identifiers: LCCN 2024040494 | ISBN 9781250206220 hardcover |
ISBN 9781250206213 ebook
Subjects: LCSH: Alabama—History | Alabama—Social conditions |
Okeowo, Alexis—Childhood and youth | African American
women—Alabama—Biography | Alabama—Biography | LCGFT:
Biographies
Classification: LCC F326 .O44 2025 | DDC 976.100496/0730092
$a B—dc23/eng/20250311
LC record available at https://lccn.loc.gov/2024040494

Our books may be purchased in bulk for promotional,
educational, or business use. Please contact your local
bookseller or the Macmillan Corporate and Premium Sales
Department at (800) 221-7945, extension 5442, or by e-mail at
MacmillanSpecialMarkets@macmillan.com.

First Edition 2025

Designed by Meryl Sussman Levavi

Printed in the United States of America

1   3   5   7   9   10   8   6   4   2

For where else? Home, and for the people who made it so.

Contents

Making a Home:
Stephanie, Brandon, Tina, and Me

Present Day:
All of Us

BLESSINGS
AND
DISASTERS

Prologue

t depends on who is doing the looking. Since the cementing of the American union, its members and borders intact, the story of Alabama has lain in its being the most visible stage for the best and worst results of our democratic experiment. But while outsiders have often glanced at the state—to draw a contrast, to make a point, to make an example of—its true nature has rarely been understood. Alabama is too racist, too religious, too backward. It either needs outside intervention or is a lost cause. And the chapters that don't fit into this hopeless story don't matter. But what happens when what is left out of the official narrative becomes too bright to ignore? When the little-known, the inconvenient, and the unexpected parts of the story are presented as the story itself, no longer the exceptions or oddities? The subjects of these strange parts, all of us Alabamians on the periphery, or who are right at the center but still unseen, could then constitute an alternate history veering into the one we accepted. The footnotes moved up into the text, the asterisks clarified right there in the sentences.

Why Alabama? What about this state has birthed the most good and evil of America's story and all that falls in between?

As a foreign correspondent who has spent the last decade writing about an often-mischaracterized continent, Africa, I'm familiar with how places can be stereotyped and neglected. But it wasn't until I started spending time in my home state after the 2016 presidential election that I saw a jarring similarity in the ways the Deep South was portrayed. I realized that the assumptions held about the region can be so unconsciously, and yet firmly, narrow that they limit our conversation about how many Americas there are, if there are indeed different Americas; what those places look like; and what their residents believe. On one of Donald Trump's visits to Alabama, in 2017, he made appeals to "our heritage" and the specialness of the state. He said he believed in the righteousness of "Alabama values." But many Alabamians seem tired of being told who they are and what they want.

If the Deep South is the essence of the nation—as Howard Zinn put it, a region that "is a distillation of those traits which are the worst (and a few which are the best) in the national character"—that could be why, when I am outside the South, I can always predict the responses of people once I tell them I am from Alabama.

I never really left the South until I graduated from high school; moving to college in New Jersey was the second time in my life I traveled by plane, the first being seven years earlier. Leaving hadn't been necessary. Every place that was important or desirable to me, from school to where we vacationed, was reachable by car, and everyone around me learned how to drive by, at the latest, the age of fifteen. My first car, which I raced from my high school parking lot to the mall to my house while blasting Three 6 Mafia, Trina, and OutKast on HOT 105.7, was my family's stop sign–red Plymouth Voyager minivan. It was so uncool my friends found it endearing. When I was growing up, my hometown of Montgomery was the source of what I knew about how people related to one another and what I could assume about a person from how they carried themselves, how they talked to me, and where they lived. The things I thought I knew—that there was always a geographic direction in which to aspire to move, that talking to everyone regardless of their schooling or money was vital to both your spiritual and your social standing, that it mattered that you let others know your educational and material statuses with grace and that you let them know what those statuses were—still felt essential when I looked back years later.

When I left the South, I was wearing the most neutral of disguises. My clothes consisted of tops and miniskirts belonging to the girl-next-door-at-the-mall aesthetic, found at stores like the Limited and Express, and I unintentionally had a characterless accent, a vaguely coastal one I could have developed because of a dissonance between the drawls of my friends and the Nigerian accents of my parents. My summer job was at a mall store called American Eagle, which I abandoned as soon as I got a job at the sexier Express. As a child, most of my travel came about when my mom, my two younger brothers, and I followed my dad to academic conferences in cities around the region, like Baton Rouge and Biloxi and Raleigh, or when we went on weekend vacations to Atlanta, the Black southerner's version of New York City. We usually stayed in my parents' favorite hotel chain, Embassy Suites, on these trips; my parents rented a one-bedroom suite with two double beds and a pull-out couch, and we fell into a sleeping arrangement that allowed us all just enough space. Around five thirty every evening during those stays, my mom, who, like my dad, usually never drank, took the elevator to the lobby to use the free drink tickets we got at check-in to pick up plastic cups of margaritas and Styrofoam bowls of trail mix. She brought the drinks and snacks back to our suite, and she and my dad drank the margaritas on the couch while watching the news and made-for-TV movies while my brothers and I stuck to the bedroom, trying not to kill one another. I got into one of the beds and read about hot cheerleaders faking their deaths and astral projection in Christopher Pike and Lois Duncan novels. While my dad was at a conference during the day, my mom, brothers, and I spent the hours lounging around the suite and walking the hotel grounds, once losing my baby brother near the tennis courts, until my dad got back, and then we would all go to the mall to visit the stores and the food court. It was unfussy, boring, relaxing. Our tastes were modest, decent. We drove from Montgomery every trip, no matter how long it took.

But I fantasized about indecency. After eighteen years of imagining the world outside the South, I arrived on the baroquely lush campus of Princeton University in the fall of 2002. I remember walking over what felt like acres of clipped, vivid green with my family, looking up at Gothic arches. We were staying in an Embassy Suites–like hotel not quite in the town of Princeton, and we had driven onto campus in our rental car to move me into my dorm.

Later, I was standing in a crowd of people from my freshman class, waiting to leave a lecture hall after orientation, in front of a boy who would become my editor at the campus alternative weekly; he was talking with his friend, who would become known as the campus coke dealer, about a girl who had brought a DVR to install in her dorm room because she couldn't miss her favorite television shows while she was in class. The boys sounded amused and impressed. They mentioned the girl's skiing vacations and her boarding school, the name of which seemed to be shorthand for a good pedigree. Her name, which was Tobin, also seemed to be shorthand for the kind of taste that preferred wealth to style. I had had no idea there were even kids who wanted to venture beyond the driving radius around their homes and go to a place like boarding school. Standing in that crowd was when I realized that many of the symbols of status I knew—summers spent at the lake, membership to the right church youth group—no longer applied and that I would soon have to learn what the new, relevant symbols were. I was sheltered by parents who had refused to let me date or go to late-night parties, but who had seen no problem in taking my brothers and me to weekend matinee showings of erotic thrillers like *Single White Female* or letting us read anything we wanted as vicarious experimentation. I needed to transition from consuming whatever adult novel I could find in the public library to expertly responding to the late-night drunken voicemails from the boy standing behind me at orientation, the lovely coke dealer. Modesty and decency were relative here.

I knew very little about Princeton before going. I zoomed in on photos of its campus on Google, examined carefully chosen images on its website to see how students were dressed and which ones were grouped together, and spent time looking around to see what people did with their days besides going to class. I never visited the campus, despite Princeton having a "Pre-Frosh Weekend." Visiting seemed too expensive, would take up too much time, and no one suggested it. After receiving my acceptance email, I celebrated for a few minutes with my parents and then went back to the computer to email the admissions office. I needed to ask how many Black students were at the school, because it was impossible to tell from the photos. It was an email I never would have sent to a school south of Virginia—the farthest north I had ever been—where I could be sure to find enough people who looked like me. In the mid-2000s, and twenty years on, the South remained the Blackest part of the country; more than half its Black population lived there as of 2022. Despite the Great Migration having taken millions of Black southerners to the North during the first

half of the twentieth century, to escape racism and terror, millions of Black people had returned to the South or
come for the first time. The Princeton admissions office
responded that African Americans made up about 9 percent of the student body; the office added that I should
let them know if I needed any more information. The percentage would have to do.

It didn't take long to realize I was an anomaly of sorts
on campus: one of not many Black students, one of not
many Black southern students, and one of not many
southern students at all. Even at a university that, by
reputation, was the most preppy-attired, conservative
values–holding, and thus "southern," of all the colleges
in the Northeast, there were few people who claimed to
belong to the last two categories. There were a lot of pastel
polo collars that stood straight up, and seersucker trousers, and miniskirts that pleated out—but mostly from
designer labels, not from the retail chains that populated
the malls in my town. There was a line of awful quilted
handbags by the designer Vera Bradley, made to look like
something your grandmother should have thrown out,
that girls with names like Tobin carried.

I wanted to troll the campus's homogeneity, its careful
niceties. I took a course taught by ultra-conservative professor Robert George, who had coauthored a proposed constitutional amendment restricting marriage to heterosexual
couples and who taught constitutional interpretation and
civil liberties. I raised my hand all the time, at almost every
lecture, to answer his questions, and I still remember his
look of slight surprise the first time it happened.

Any comfort I took in Princeton's reputation as a

southern-minded school was supposed to make me feel
better that I was one of a handful of students in my high
school class leaving Alabama; college would be something
like home far from home. So when I met other students
and professors, and we introduced ourselves, it took a
while to get used to the routine. Their reactions, depending on how much time they had spent down South,
would head down one of two distinct avenues. If they
hadn't lived lower than the Carolinas, they'd say "Alabama?!" with outright surprise or, if they were able to fix
their expressions soon enough, a "Whoa, Alabama" with
careful wariness. As I confirmed they had heard me right,
they seemed to be imagining the extremity of what being
a Black girl from Alabama must entail. Fire hoses, lynchings. Then a "What was *that* like?" with the dumbstruck
look still on their faces, sometimes shaking their heads
with pity for troubles assumed to have been endured. If
they were from the South, there was usually an assumption that we would get along, an easiness that I returned
in kind. But that didn't happen often. Any college Republicans I ran into were from Connecticut or New Jersey.

It was difficult—is still difficult—to look head-on at
Alabama; it was uncomfortable. It was also easier for
most people to believe they were more sure about my
home state than I was. Alabama was where I had learned
how to think and decide what I valued. But their expec-
tations about how I grew up pushed me to choose a
side: either agree and play up the state's worst aspects
or weakly defend it. So much so that, over time, I began
to forget parts of how I had grown up, the nuances of
how Alabamians lived and thought, and could recall

only broad strokes about race and politics and religion. I began to forget that Alabama is, before anything else, home.

Those people and I weren't ready for what lay in between: the worth of a place and why people choose to call it home. Why do people stay? And what happens to them? Alabama was the best place to find the answers.

Beginning

n the South they are convinced that they are capable of having bloodied their land with history," Joan Didion wrote, one of the observations from her brief, glancing journal of travels in the Deep South that felt true. The land in Alabama is made up of layers of soil tinted red and brown and black, enriched with clay, sand, iron, and the remains of whoever lived on and fought to stay on it at the time. A primary reason hazard-yellow and hell-red signs gleam from the creamy earth and from the peeling bases of trees is the recognition of that willingly and unwillingly sacrificed blood and the acceptance that it could be necessary to shed some of your own. One of my family's greatest achievements was when my parents bought our first house and could tend to and protect the land under it. Nobody could fuck with our property, and our neighbors felt the same about theirs. To this day, when I visit my parents' current house, I am aware that their neighbors are casually, but keenly, keeping an eye on the goings-on of the sidewalks and streets from their curtained windows. My parents like to watch out their windows, too.

When I was in elementary school, couldn't have been more than ten or eleven, I caught sight of our snake. It was black with red markings, I think—I saw it for only a second—and its body was dense, coils of gleaming flesh. It emerged from the neon green of the low-cut grass in my family's backyard, right near the fence guarding our plot of land from the street. I stood still as it poked out of the depths of the earth, then disappeared almost as quickly, burying itself in the grass and dirt again. I was frozen for a moment longer and then ran into the house to pull my dad outside. The snake was gone. My dad gave me a reassuring squeeze of the shoulder; I had probably imagined it, he said. I started to protest and then stopped. It was a weird thing to happen in the groomed tranquility of our front lawn—I hardly believed I had seen it. We both looked across the street.

The family living in the house opposite ours was the bane of my father's domestic existence: the yard he worked hard to cultivate, the home he made sure was always clean. Their house was just like ours—attractive, modest, plucked from a suburban mail-order catalog. But their front lawn was a disaster: toys and bicycles in varying states of disrepair, discarded lawn equipment, and occasionally trash. I thought the family was nice: they had a couple of kids, some of whom used to come over to play video games with my brothers and me. My dad tolerated them. They were Black, like most of our neighbors, in a part of town that was Black. We lived in South Montgomery, where many working- and middle-class Black residents lived. A lot of the white people on the south side who could afford to leave had been fleeing for the newer subdivisions on Montgomery's east side. (And when Black people followed them east, they picked up and went farther east, right out of town, and annexed new townships. Black people followed them there, too.)

We had started off well with the neighbors across the street: my dad sometimes drove their kids to school, and everybody generally got along. But as my dad's tolerance for the sight of their yard and their domestic dramas lessened, and our neighbors' annoyance at his frustration increased, their mutual uneasiness fell in line with the tensions that can arise between Black immigrants and Black Americans.

My family is also Black American, of course. But our origin story is different from the family across the street. My mother and father immigrated separately to the United States from different parts of Nigeria and then met as college students in the close social circle of West Africans at Alabama State University, a Historically Black College in Montgomery. They were simultaneously part of and outside the Black/white racial binary that has long defined the state (replacing the Native/settler binary that burned into the humidity sometime after Alabama joined the union in 1819 and removed most of its Native residents by putting them onto the Trail of Tears). My parents and their friends were familiar and foreign, Black but other, an insular world unto themselves in Alabama in the 1970s. In those muggy days at the end of the fever of the civil rights movement, amid desegregation and increasing globalization and competition for students, public universities in the Deep South were offering financial aid to the most eager and unsuspecting: Black Africans. My parents had hesitations, but they went.

They existed along the fault line of a shared white and Black distrust of Black foreigners. But they had seen opportunity in Alabama and seized it; my brothers and I had to do the same. It was a ruthless stance: sacrifice and discipline bred success. We had pride in knowing we also belonged to a Nigerian story that predated our American one, and that was our refuge. When my parents each first moved to Alabama—my mother directly from southern Nigeria, my dad after a year at a private college in Berkeley, California—they had coinciding perceptions of the state. My dad couldn't afford another year at his college, so he opened a directory of state schools and landed on one of the first on the list. He knew Alabama had ongoing racial troubles, but he saw a chance to get an education relatively cheaply. My mom's sister was already attending college in Alabama, and my mother saw it as a place where she could, too, while being near family. They found that education, along with friends, kids, apartments, cars. Those things also became a refuge. They plunged into Alabama blind and surfaced with a new home.

In the summer of 1860, 110 other West Africans landed in Alabama blind and stunned. After being marched for thousands of miles from the interior of the continent by slave traders belonging to the Kingdom of Dahomey, they and over seventy of their kinsmen and women had arrived on the West African coast beaten and hurt and grieving. Catastrophe had struck them in a single night. Dahomian warriors had invaded their town, slaughtering many of their relatives and neighbors. The slavers planted their victims' heads on stakes and lit them on fire. The survivors were chained together and led to where water swallowed the land. It is likely many of them were Yoruba, the same ethnic group as my father's people. There were farmers, traders, at least one nobleman. Husbands, wives, and parents who would never stop grieving the people they were forced to leave behind. Once the captive men, women, and children got to the shores of the Atlantic Ocean, a ship's captain from Alabama was waiting for them. His name was William Foster, and he was piloting a ship called the *Clotilda*. The United States had legally banned the international slave trade over fifty years before, and the Deep South needed more bodies. Foster conspired with a pair of brothers from the city of Mobile, on Alabama's Gulf Coast, for one last slave run.

One of the Meaher brothers had a plantation at Magazine Point, on a southern bend of the state. The 110 enslaved West Africans were put to work on that plantation and others, reduced from real, human existence to the degradation, humiliation, and violence of slavery— and were likely equally disoriented when, five years later, slavery legally ended and the Civil War was over. Did they know there was a war? Records seem to indicate they didn't. They were "free" again, a state of the mind and soul they still felt, despite having been treated as things. Because they had been in Alabama only five years, they set about trying to go home. It was not an unrealistic possibility. Communities of once-enslaved Africans had returned from Brazil and Cuba to their homes in West Africa. But with no help from the Meahers, the West Africans in Alabama found themselves stuck. So they created a place of their own. "If they were going to stay in Alabama, it had to be on their own terms," as Sylviane A. Diouf writes in *Dreams of Africa in Alabama*.

Edged on three sides by the Mobile River, a wild bayou, and Three Mile Creek (the same waters that first carried them up to the Meaher plantation), the free West Africans founded their community in 1866 as African Town. It is now known as Africatown, a quarter in the southern port city of Mobile, and its bones are the same: the plots of land the West Africans tirelessly worked and saved for, the simple houses and church and school they built themselves, the gardens they farmed—all amid the constant racial terrorism that took many of their descendants. Africatown was a community, the first of many to come in Alabama, "expressive of African ingenuity and a prime model of the processes of African acculturation in the American South—a haven from white supremacy and ostracism of Black Americans," as Deborah G. Plant writes in her introduction to Zora Neale Hurston's *Barracoon*.

Decades of joy and heartbreak followed emancipation as the free West Africans tried to raise families under hostile state surveillance, in a place that had used them, and then had no idea what to do with them. Their Black

American neighbors often treated them with disdain and hostility, out of ignorance and fear, and stayed away from them; their children were called savages and cannibals at school.

Soon after my parents met in Alabama, they left. My father graduated from college, and they moved to Tennessee and then Texas to pursue their respective graduate degrees. I was born and spent the first six months of my life in Houston. I have no memories of the city, and when I think of it, my mind goes to the one story I have ever heard of our time there.

We lived in an apartment complex with a glimmering turquoise pool, and, despite not knowing how to swim, my dad confidently jumped in one afternoon. The water just looked too inviting. He immediately started to thrash around as my mom watched in panic. But my dad managed to pull himself out and then lay on the concrete, dazed. Houston, I was to understand, almost swallowed us alive until we got ourselves out and went home; my mom laughed deliriously whenever she told the story.

After leaving Texas and spending a couple of years back in Tennessee, my parents decided it was time to return to Alabama. They have been there ever since. A teaching job for my dad at Alabama State and their old community were calling. I was six at that point, but Montgomery is the only place I consider my hometown, the place where the bare bones of my self grew and fused together and gently solidified. All that came after would spring from this place.

* * *

On a map, Alabama appears compact, a trapezoid with a foot dragging lazily—or provocatively, depending on the looker's mood—at its southwestern edge, into the big blue Gulf gnawing at it from below. On the ground, Alabama feels enormous, taking drivers on rides that last several hours from one end to the other, even though it's 52,423 square miles, just the thirtieth-largest state. I spent nearly all my childhood in Montgomery, in the flat central expanse, two-thirds of the way down to Florida from the northern border with Tennessee and one-third of the way to Mississippi from the eastern line with Georgia. It is now a city of, give or take, two hundred thousand people that is so obsessed with its past that its downtown, its conflicted and confused heart, is openly having an identity crisis. Downtown is never that busy: in the sole part of town where people walk instead of drive, office workers still wait for green lights before crossing the road, even when there is no traffic. Its generous street grid, all wide sidewalks and fat car lanes, is frequently interrupted by beloved landmarks like the Rosa Parks Museum and the Civil Rights Memorial.

A century and a half ago, those same streets were lined with warehouses and markets for enslaved people. (In 1860, two-thirds of the city's population was enslaved.) In the years of the 2020s, I can stroll less than a block from the pale columns of the Alabama State Capitol with the state flag, white with a red diagonal cross in homage to the Confederacy, waving above, to a two-story white wooden frame house with green shutters called the First White House of the Confederacy, built in 1861 and moved to its present location during a neighborhood renovation in

1921. Jefferson Davis, former president of the Confederacy, once resided there. A statue of him rises over marble steps leading up to the capitol—Alabama marble, said to be the whitest in the world, plucked from Talladega County, about a two hours' drive north of Montgomery. I can then stop in a museum on the Freedom Riders, about seven blocks on west. I can double back to the capitol and, before arriving, go worship at an orange-brick-and-white-trim church with the name of Dexter Avenue King Memorial Baptist, where Martin Luther King Jr. served as pastor. I can next walk past an eighty-eight-foot-tall cylindrical statue shooting straight into the sky called the Alabama Confederate Monument, meant to honor thousands of Confederate soldiers fallen during the Civil War. I can go for oysters in a sleek restaurant and then get down-home fried chicken around the corner for half the price. The past is so present that it overpowers it, certainly by design.

Like most other capitals in the Deep South, Montgomery has annexed its green exteriors into yawning rings of subdivisions and independent-minded townships. There is nature outside the city limits, but the part inside has become fake: the garish and bristly greens of overwatered lawns and golf courses; the aquamarine blues in clunky fountains and manmade lakes; and the soft, gray sweeps of courts and drives and other words for "street" designed to make the southern homeowner feel at home. When I go for a run in my parents' neighborhood these days, I pass a man-made pond where residents go fishing—and are then required to throw back their toxic catch—and a fountain that always refracts a perfect rainbow when the sunlight collides with the water. The concrete glares and the sun beats down and the grass prickles and dark water sometimes runs into the gutters along the streets. It all feels cheerily artificial. It also does feel like home; it looks like the setting for all the warmest houses I ever spent time in growing up. But I have to get out of town to really get outside.

Much of the state is still radiantly green, despite industrialization and deforestation. Its thickets of forest cover well over half the state, and farms carpet over a fifth of it. Out in the country, you can imagine how the border between urban and rural was once tenuous. The green in Alabama is tangible, something that can be held on to: the grasses, trees, bushes, and other verdant outgrowths from the ground are, often all at once, scratchy and smooth and giving. Demanding to be touched, grabbed, pulled. Alabamians have done all these things, its Native inhabitants and colonial pioneers and enslaved people and farmers and field laborers and migrant workers exploring and prodding and pushing around for their next meal or home or riches. The green is part of the Alabamian psyche. It is the best of what we have to show for ourselves, our natural and God-given blessings. It is the source material for what has made the state great—the waterways and foliage that encouraged foraging and settlement and made way for sustenance, the crops that gave rise to a heady plantation economy and then churning farms, and the dense soil underfoot that has persisted through plunder and upheaval. The green is the sign of our survival, that we made it, and will keep making it, past what keeps seeming like the worst.

The green is in the fields full of cattle, where kids used to go cow tipping in the 1990s, and before, and collapsed into the grass drunk with laughter. Thirty minutes northwest of Montgomery is the Sunflower Field: twenty-five acres of farmland in the town of Autaugaville planted every year with half a million buttery flowers that attract tourists in the summer. Going to the northern reaches of the state from Montgomery is my favorite drive. Along the way, the green lightens and darkens, shimmers and explodes into sky. Taking I-65 north to Birmingham means passing the light fluorescent green grass in short and neat clusters running alongside the interstate until reaching the furry hills and mountains of the north. The dark-haired Appalachian Mountains, which swivel up out of the state into Tennessee, roam near several other mountains, like Cheaha and Bald Rock, none particularly high or renowned. A plateau that laps the state, called the Cumberland, is flat and high in the north and is run through with tributaries of the Tennessee River. The interstate takes me up in elevation without letting me know how much higher I have traveled; it is only when I exit the highway and head into town that I realize I am now rounding the skirt of a mountain, on a road where drivers navigate its fluctuating widths and curves at full speed with the casualness of ordering a chicken plate.

If I, instead, drive south out of my hometown, I eventually hit a forested coastal plain that rolls west into Mississippi and rolls on even deeper toward the Gulf of Mexico. Before I get far, I reach the town of Wetumpka, just outside Montgomery, the site of Alabama's most famous (to Alabamians) natural disaster: a thousand-foot meteorite crashed there scores of millions of years ago, imprinting a five-mile-wide crater into the hills. Keep going south toward Mobile, a two-and-half-hour drive from the capital, and marshland and swamps sprout along the coast of the Gulf and mosey on into Florida. Keep going and find the beaches, convenient to Mardi Gras celebrations in Mobile, where revelers toss beads and Moon Pies from parade floats but nudity is discouraged. Beyond the vibrating, dark blue vista of the sea are the Caribbean and the Atlantic. I learned to swim at the YMCA in Montgomery as a college student one summer, with my baby brother George. We obediently held our breaths, ducked under the aquamarine water, and pushed our hands out to glide. We jumped off the diving board strapped into lifejackets. We were the oldest people there, except for the white mothers sitting at a table nearby, who smiled and sized me up in my one-piece bathing suit whenever I walked around the pool. I realized that despite my fear of being consumed by water, I loved being around it.

The state flower is the camellia, sugary pink and red and sometimes considered difficult to grow, which blooms in the winter and spring, and the state bird is the cartoon-like yellowhammer, a chunky woodpecker that likes to nest in dead or dying trees. The soldiers from Alabama who died and did not die during the Civil War were nicknamed Yellowhammers because of the gray and yellow of their uniforms, and their home became known as the Yellowhammer State. Acres of farms all over the state grow peaches and pecans and, to a much lesser extent, blackberries—it's the state fruit anyway—the crops that modern Alabama is most known for, and some family farms still grow cotton, the crop the state will always be known for. In the 1860s, more cotton was shipped out of Mobile than any other city in the world except New Orleans. In 1914, it grew on nearly four million acres in Alabama. In 2017, it was down to 435,000 acres. Now the state ranks at about the middle of the seventeen others still producing cotton. Planting begins in April, and harvest before the gloom of November.

Alabama is steamy in spring and summer and often fall, sticky limbs and burning car interiors, and then the temperature cools to a mild chill in winter. In the state's central parts it rarely snows, and when it does, towns shut down, schools and offices and businesses, as public services attempt to figure out what to do amid the inch or two that falls and sticks. Manufacturing is how the state earns its money, making cars and planes. The state is the third-highest producer of cars in the nation due to automotive manufacturing plants belonging to the likes of Mercedes-Benz, where staff voted against unionizing in 2024. Amazon has several warehouses in the state, including one in Bessemer, where staff also thought about unionizing in 2021 and 2022, but didn't.

Stretches of land in the north that once flowered cotton have been converted into factory parks and subdivisions of family-size houses with green grassy squares for residents who work at the plants or commute to jobs in places like Huntsville and Decatur. South of these two cities, Birmingham has over a million residents in its metro and suburban areas, several colleges, a mall with stores that can also be found in Atlanta and New York, a busy downtown, and a cultural life. It also has bloating halos of wealthy white suburbs receding into the iron ore curtain of Red Mountain, which looms over the city. The city has long had these features, the clear signs of cosmopolitanism to a child who lived in the less exciting capital and who was buried in novels about the world, but its center has taken on a hipster aesthetic, with art spaces and cafés and acclaimed restaurants; the *New York Times* put it on its must-visit list in 2017. An hour and a half south, in Montgomery, we had, while I was growing up in the 1990s, a Shakespearean theater and an art museum and Old Alabama Town, where reenactors in period dress from the nineteenth and early twentieth centuries wandered in and out of rustic antebellum homes as they taught schoolchildren how our ancestors lived—at least the ones who wore that kind of dress and lived in that kind of home. We listened and nodded as we eyed the stalls selling rock candy. Eventually, Montgomery would try to update itself, too, getting a restored waterfront and a row of fun bars downtown, along with a gay-friendly spot where, folks gossiped, the most famous TV weatherman in town had been sighted more than once.

CHAPTER ONE

The First

When your home is on land that has been turned over so many times, changed character depending on the circumstances, been in dispute as to who owns it, there is value in claiming to be the first. Here before anyone else intruded, the original inheritors of an earth that always looks better when looking back. (Alabama loves nothing more than looking back.) Being first is the easiest kind of authority available when you have little other power, and telling someone to go back to where they came from is one of the foremost assertions of that authority. If an outsider doesn't like what is going on, they should go, leave Alabama to those who know it best and what's best for it—except we're still not entirely honest about who came first and what exactly happened to them.

Before the U.S. government partially carved Alabama

out of 21 million acres taken from tribes that once made a home on them, and named it for a tribe that lived on its central range, this land belonged to the Muscogee. The tribe is believed to have settled in what is now Alabama and Georgia in the mid-sixteenth century. As hunters and foragers, the Muscogee were drawn to land near the plentiful sources of water, the creeks and rivers, where they could grow food—corn, beans, squash, sweet potatoes, pumpkins, and melons—and make a home. More than any other natural feature of the area, the waterways were paramount, a source of nourishment and cleansing, a way to move both people and things. Muscogee towns and farmsteads could always be found near streams and swamps and the animal life that resided in and around them. Their wet green was "home to an incredible number of waterfowl, including varieties of herons, cranes, storks, ibises, ducks, and geese," as Robbie Ethridge writes in *Creek Country: The Creek Indians and Their World*.

The Alabama, Natchez, Tuskegee, and other tribes who lost to the Muscogee in battle became part of their nation, a union that valued kin. The Muscogee were seen as "fierce fighters, yet generous to those whom they conquered," Lou Vickery notes in *The Rise of the Poarch Band of Creek Indians*. Within the nation, there were also tribes who sought refuge after devastation from disease or from the European slave trade in Indians; Indians from neighboring tribes who had married in; settlers from Spain, France, and England; and settlers born on American soil. Women did the farming, and men the commercial hunting and ranching. In the matriarchal tradition, when a man married a woman, he moved with his wife to live among her clan, where they raised their family. The children then belonged to the clan of their mother, and her male relatives helped rear them. The father aided with the domestic decisions of his own sisters' families. The state's original family values.

The Muscogee believed that animal spirits created the earth and that people needed to live in harmony with those spirits. The Indians resided amid forests of oak, hickory, and pine and on the plains of tall grasses that sprang from the dark, mushy soil of the Black Belt. Their medicines came from plants and trees and bushes, like red root, for fever and pain, and river birch, for cleansing. The Muscogee claimed this land, taking from it plenty, through deerskin trading and cattle and hog raising. They had no written language; they prized oratory and storytelling. When European explorers first encountered the Muscogee in the seventeenth century, they began to call them the Creek, because of their proximity to the water. At the end of the century, the Creek held expanses of territory mostly in Alabama and Georgia, and the tribe could spread their hands and touch the Tombigbee River in Alabama all the way to the Oconee River in Georgia. Lower Creek made homes on the tails of the Chattahoochee and Flint Rivers in Georgia, and Upper Creek resided in the valleys of the Coosa, Tallapoosa, and Alabama Rivers in Alabama, near what is now Montgomery. The European settlers, the new Americans, and their nascent union called this Indian nation of some twenty thousand people the Creek Confederacy.

When I was very young, Indian communities in the state were in the local news during various stages of their struggles for sovereignty, which were often not victorious, and nearly every Black kid I knew in elementary school claimed to have "some Indian" in them, but the Creek as a people and an identity felt foreign to me. Native Americans lived up in Oklahoma and the Midwest, according to school history lessons; they had nothing much to do with Alabama. Once I learned, years after I graduated from the Montgomery County public school system, how the Creek Nation had been forced into and then survived the state, it was as if a simultaneous reality had revealed itself. I began to see live evidence of the tribe, who now called themselves the Poarch Band of Creek Indians, everywhere: on billboards, in newspaper ads, and on highway exit signs advertising their businesses. I was watching TV with my parents during dinner when a commercial for the tribe once came on, showing young multiracial children making crafts and telling viewers that they cared about family values. "Alabama natives," went the slogan on the tribe's website, "Alabama neighbors." The photo above the phrase showed a man with light brown skin, presumably Creek, wearing a flared sand-colored cowboy hat. *We are just like you*, the tribe was saying, *and we might be even more what you think you are than you are*. It was both reassurance and challenge. As I drove slowly through the Poarch Creek Indian Reservation in the southern green of the state for the first time in 2018, it seemed both like I was in a foreign country and, with its prickly and unhurried rurality, in the most Alabamian of places I had ever been.

It is a disorienting kind of existence to be Native and Alabamian, Indian and southern. In the 1970s, a Creek

girl named Stephanie Bryan felt this experience intimately. I first met Stephanie in 2018, after looking up
the Poarch Creek's tribal council on their website. In the
center of a photo filled with mostly older, white-passing
men was a petite middle-aged woman with lightly olive
skin, dark hair just past her shoulders, and the smile of a
proud mom. Various photos on the site showed her with
crossed arms in a dark suit and red lipstick, smiling; in a
white button-down shirt with the sleeves slightly rolled
up and gold jewelry, talking to children and elderly people, smiling; and in a bright red blouse in front of a slot
machine in a casino, still smiling. I was surprised to see
her and immediately felt she was the member whose
story I wanted to hear. After a few emails exchanged
with the tribe's press contact, Stephanie and I set an interview date, and I was looking up the reservation on Google
Maps. I had never heard about the Poarch Creek in history classes, never seen memorials devoted to them downtown. All the while, the tribe had been warring with the
state to exercise their sovereignty; Alabama was resisting
them every step of the way. When I drove down to visit
Stephanie on the reservation, she talked about Jesus and
love so often that I could almost forget she was the one
fighting the latest battles as the tribe's first female leader.

Stephanie was hard to miss on their reservation as a
girl, full cheeks with a head of dark, curly hair and a gentle drawl. She grew up right near her tribe's powwow
grounds, which at the time held the reservation's only
community building; it was the core of their rez. Kids
were always out on the grassy grounds playing kickball,
dodgeball, stickball, and screaming with glee. Stephanie

saw kids in school, white kids who clearly came from richer families, and she studied the things they had: better pencils and markers and notebooks and clothes and shoes. She felt her difference when those same kids singled out her and the others from the rez by not inviting them to their birthday and pool parties. Her tribe was poor, had been poor for as long as she could remember and long before that. "The ancestors and what they experienced in life was not the greatest" was how Stephanie said it to me. Her grandmother Lunie Mae told her about the days when the tribe had even less, when she couldn't ride the school buses because they were reserved for white students and people spat at her and other Poarch kids and insulted them with slurs. In 1939, the Episcopal Church had opened a school for the Poarch, but it was lacking in supplies and funding. Just over ten years later, the county finally built a public elementary school in their community. Poarch kids were also finally able to go to the public high school in town, mixing for the first time with their white peers. None of it had come easy, but it had resulted in Stephanie, some two decades later, going to public school in Atmore, her drowsy hometown in southern Alabama.

By the end of the 1970s, when Stephanie was in elementary school, the Poarch Creek were a people in crisis. The tribe practically functioned like a family—Stephanie's grandfather had served on the tribal council, and so had her uncle—but the time had arrived to make sure their tribe was seen and treated as more than just an extended clan, both for their sake and the sake of their descendants to come. The Poarch Creek were kin and country, the sur-

vivors of the worst events that can befall a people, from
displacement to near eradication. And for over a century,
the federal government had treated them alternately like
an extra finger or a phantom limb: Indian tribes were
either a blot on the national union, a stain that refused
to go away and that scarred a pristine origin story of
discovery and conquest; or a nearly forgotten remnant, a
part of the story its tellers preferred to leave out. Reparations for the trespasses against the Poarch Creek would
take many forms, some of the most crucial unknowable
in those days, but the most fundamental one was clear to
all in the tribe—their independence. Federal recognition
of their sovereignty, that holy grail desired by the survivors of tribes all over Indian country, would put into law
what the Poarch Creek had known all their lives. They
were Alabama, the first in the truest sense, and also apart
from it, a thread of the state's narrative that anchored its
beginnings but was distinct and proud and unwilling to
assimilate. That pride and defiance would be their way
to freedom, or their undoing.

When Stephanie was growing up, the roads that kids ran
down barefoot were still dirt; the buildings still wooden.
Stephanie got her teeth cleaned in an Airstream bus that
came through the rez every few months. They had enough
to eat and a community where everyone looked out for
one another, so there was that, but not much else. Stephanie's grandmother taught her early on that if white
people insulted her, not to let it bother her. The Poarch
Creek knew who they were, probably more than any other
people in the twenty-two square miles of space the tribe
shared with their neighbors in town. Stephanie's mom,

Julia Ann, worked three jobs and raised Stephanie and her two brothers and two sisters alone; Stephanie was the baby of the family. Well, that's not right. Julia Ann raised Stephanie with her own mom, Lunie Mae, and with her sister Marie, a knot of women who cared for Stephanie and paid her mind. Lunie Mae lived with them, had done so since the year her husband, Buck, died and Stephanie was born. Lunie Mae served on the tribal education committee and volunteered at the rez school, where she worked in the kitchen. She also worked at a carpet store and a barbecue shack. Lunie Mae seemed impossibly strong. Stephanie watched her.

Stephanie's uncle Otha lived behind their house and was a kind of father to her. (She never knew her biological father, who left when she was small.) A garden separated their homes, and her uncle let her help tend it. It felt special to plant the seeds and, if she made sure to water and care for them, to watch the corn and okra grow. Stephanie relished being in the green with him in the sun, pulling weeds and hauling the five-gallon water buckets and feeling like she was contributing to her community. When the fruits and vegetables grew in, she helped take them first to the elders, running up to their doors with the bounty. Elders are important to the Poarch Creek, and the ones Stephanie grew up with had experienced much of the pain that had fallen on people like them "when it wasn't cool to be Indian," Stephanie said—although it hadn't yet become cool during her childhood, either. She started thinking sooner than many about what it meant to have a wealth that wasn't material, about what sustained her people when they were told to go back to where they came from.

Stephanie had no idea what she wanted to be when she got older, as the rez was not a place where people had high career aspirations, but she sensed her life would have something to do with helping people. She took to heart what the preacher in her church said: *Be good to your neighbors, give them a hand when they need it*. She was quieter than the rest, but she did believe she loved people, and she tried to love the classmates who wondered aloud about the poor Poarch girl who kept to herself. Stephanie got Indian public assistance in the form of extra tutoring, and everybody in class knew it because, every year, the teachers would ask who was Indian, and the Native students had to raise their hands. Stephanie tried to put hers up with confidence.

Not long after she turned twelve, Stephanie's family encouraged her to compete for the title of Poarch Creek Princess, and she agreed. Princesses have to represent the tribe in the most uplifting and wholesome way possible, set a strong example for young Indians. As part of the contest, each girl has to have a traditional calico dress made, with an apron and moccasins, and take basket weaving and basic Creek language and history lessons. They learn traditional dances and have to prove they can speak publicly. Stephanie won. Still, she begged her older sister Ruthie to accept the crown on her behalf because she was too embarrassed to get up in front of everyone. But a crown suited her.

Stephanie and I were in the center for assisted living on the rez, where her office was located for the time being. The center had been renovated in recent years. While I was waiting for her in the lobby, I sat under an exposed wooden beam ceiling and looked at the people milling around the spacious room, at the open fireplace and the courtyard outside. The place felt true to the cultural reverence for elders Stephanie would mention. The tribal intent seemed to be that as people on the rez aged, they would be taken care of with dignity and respect. Given that Nigerians treat their elders the same, I could relate. While Stephanie was telling me her story later in a meeting room, I got the vivid sense that she was trying both to follow talking points and to make sure I understood the reason for her lines. It was a performance, but it had enough sincerity to be appealing, even sympathetic.

Stephanie has become successful, a politician and businesswoman whose goal is to ensure more success for her people—and so, someone I knew not to fully trust. Her tribe has prevailed, built a billion-dollar gambling empire, but they still think of themselves as the underdog. For them, it is about having the kind of wealth that means no one can ever tell them what to do with it or what to do, period. It was imperative to Stephanie that I know that the tribe had been the first, but that they weren't holding it against anybody. They just wanted what was owed them: freedom to determine their lives just like everybody else. In that way, they are utterly Alabamian. Because as much we claim we don't need unfair advantages, a free ride, we also believe in getting what is owed to us. Which seems to be everything. In Alabama, I encounter more people, of all races and age groups, on federal disability benefits, for injuries sometimes hard to discern, than anywhere else I have been. The state has the second-highest number of people in the country on disability. But when it comes to its own money, Alabama is consistently among the least generous of the states when paying welfare benefits: $215 a month for a family of three, as of 2023, less than half the national monthly median of $492.

For all her seeming difference, Stephanie is a vision of southern femininity. Whenever I saw her, she wore lipstick and delicate jewelry, and her dark hair was curled. She radiates the kind of steeliness masked with perfect manners that I associate with the moms of my white childhood friends. Gracious, but deadly if crossed. Her energy is occasionally maternal. I alternately felt wary in her presence and wanting of her approval. Whenever she mentioned race, she made sure to look me in the eye: "My parents, my grandparents, always instilled in me to treat others the way you want to be treated, no matter their race, and I treat everybody the same. I think that if we, this whole nation, would go back to the four-letter word, as referenced so much in the Bible—and that's 'love.' Love one another, help thy neighbor."

In so many respects, Stephanie looks like a descendant of the "mixed-blood" Creek who, in 1813, helped the U.S. government battle Creek warriors opposed to European expansion onto Native land: pale skin, hazel eyes, just the hint of a darker undertone to her complexion. Not long after the Creek Confederacy came in contact with Europeans, it started to splinter. The Creek were divided over what to do with the white settlers, whose intrusions onto their land were growing more invasive and troubling with each new trade route and residential settlement.

A federal road, built in 1805, snaked through the green between the Chattahoochee and Alabama Rivers, from what is now Athens, Georgia, to present-day Mobile. It was intended to make mail delivery easier between Washington and New Orleans. Six years later, that mail path became a war road. Settlers were disregarding borders and crossing onto Creek land to hunt, fish, farm, cut timber, graze livestock, and build homesteads, creating tension and conflict between the two groups. Many Creek were opposed to the white settlers' encroachment, and their warriors, called Red Sticks, would decide to fight to defend their land from federal government forces. But others, who became known as the Friendly Creek, didn't want war. These included a wealthy minority who had enough to lose, like their sunburned ranches on the Tensaw River north of Mobile, lucrative trade in logging and farm crops, cattle that roamed. Most of the wealthy were of mixed racial heritage—"some wealthier, lighter-skinned Creeks managed to retain some of the rich bottomlands near Tensaw. Their history gradually diverged from their darker-skinned, 'Indian-looking' brethren," as Mark Edwin Miller puts it in *Claiming Tribal Identity*. The original elders of the Poarch Band of Creek Indians were among them.

By 1811, the Creek Confederacy had splintered, and by 1813, war had begun. The Indians were never destined to win the Creek War. Red Stick warriors couldn't compete with the federal government's star general, Andrew Jackson, and his troops, who were working with the Friendly Creek and other Indian tribes. (The Friendly Creek had to wear pale feathers in their hair to avoid friendly fire from their white partners during battle, which still happened anyway.) Jackson defeated the last Red Stick fighters at the Battle of Horseshoe Bend. He razed their towns, and the surviving warriors, with their families, sought refuge on Seminole land, down in Florida, where they would continue resisting. The remaining Creek were refugees, starving in the Alabama woods or accepting food from U.S. forces. Even the Friendly Creek lost their property and livestock and would spend much of the rest of their lives trying to hold on to the inferior replacement land the federal government gave them.

The Treaty of Fort Jackson ended the Creek War in 1814. For the Friendly Creek, the most valuable part of the treaty was the land it promised them. The U.S. Supreme Court soon decided that the Creek would hold land at the discretion of the federal government. Once they selected their plots of land, the government would reserve them for the tribe. The first federal reservations. True ownership was now a thing of the past. But their old settlement, the fertile strip of land on the Tensaw River, was no longer available. White settlers had already claimed much of it. A Friendly Creek named Lynn McGhee, whose mother was Creek and his father a Scottish trader, was given 640 acres in gratitude for his acting as a guide for General Jackson during the war. He was said to have saved Jackson's life at the Battle of Horseshoe Bend. McGhee cast around for a suitable place and landed on Red Hill, less than two dozen miles inland from the Tensaw. Several Creek families—the Moniacs, the Rolins, the Weatherfords, and others—would go on to make the area their home. In 1836, Congress agreed to pass an act allowing Lynn McGhee; his wife, Hattie Semioce; and another Friendly Creek to claim reserved land in the state to make up for the property they lost during the war. McGhee was distinguishing himself as a leader. A government agent dispatched to Indian country described him as "a half breed in the savannas . . . who is of an excellent character, speaks English well."

Alabama had marked the cloudy Coosa River as the eastern border between the state and what was left of the Creek Confederacy when it entered the union in 1819. But settlers were destroying the Creek's homesteads and threatening their lives to force them to turn over their land. The Creek have a word for those who came for their homes: *ecunnaunuxulgee*, or "those greedily grasping after our lands." Many Creek families had no choice but to leave their homes with just what they could carry. Settlers took their place. These were the squatter claims. Settlers also cheated a number of others out of what they owned. These were many of the land sales. In 1832, the Creek signed a treaty with the federal government to divide their land into individual properties for tribe members, 320 acres for each family and 640 acres for each chief. Families could choose to stay on their land and follow Alabama state law or relocate to Indian Territory in Oklahoma. Many stayed, until they couldn't.

But at a time when Indians were being forced off their lands, McGhee and his fellow Creek on Red Hill kept holding on to theirs. This community of a few dozen Indians filed depositions in court concerning the property stolen from them by ravaging settlers. They persuaded the U.S. government to pass special acts recognizing the losses they had experienced when their ranches were destroyed, and they used the last political and social capital they had to stay afloat on shifting ground, calling in whatever influence they had. Those records would later prove useful. Stephanie had always understood that the survival of her ancestors was due to their being successful traders, adept at building business and diplomatic relationships. They also zigzagged along the uncharted crossroads of being Indian and Alabamian with the bravado of an outsider and the heaviness of an insider who had seen too much.

The only Indians in Alabama who would survive with their tribal identity both alive and federally recognized was the clan of mixed-blood Creek who had placed their bets on siding with the U.S. government. They avoided the fate of the fourteen thousand Creek who were forced to migrate across the Mississippi, which included more than three thousand of their brethren who died along the way, on what historians have called a death march. The *Encyclopedia of American Indian Removal* says there were about a "dozen friendly Creek mixed bloods who escaped" removal and managed to cling to the land and survive. By 1845, only a small number of Creek—and their enslaved Africans—still lived in Alabama and Georgia, and over the next five years, many of those would be pushed out, too. When the Civil War ended in 1865, the loss meant not just that they could no longer own people, but that their economic future, already damaged by dispossession, was further in limbo.

The Creek in Alabama were familiar with accommodating. Some had fought alongside their white neighbors for the state, for the Confederacy. Not for the white race, exactly, and maybe not even for slavery, fully, but for their own future prospects, likely, and for self-preservation, certainly. If Alabama could not govern itself as it wanted, the Creek might not be able to, either. Their descendants had made their way to the frontier of the Gulf Coast plains, shaded by groves of pine and oak, far enough north of Mobile to feel like they were on their own. They went from being self-sustaining farmers who hunted and fished, to working in the local timber industry, to then sharecropping and doing fieldwork. They made little money, could not afford to go to school in significant numbers, and could never seem to advance; they faced discrimination at almost every step. But they stuck together, and they had managed to stay.

Alabama tried to remove all its first inhabitants, but traces of them are still everywhere: in the names of streets and neighborhoods and towns and schools, in the signs that identify boat and foot crossings. Towns with names like "Ecunchate" and "Pauwocte" once seeded and swanned along the Alabama River. The green was thicker when Indians resided on it, possessed species that no longer exist, like the groves of reedy bamboo grasses called canebrakes that coated hundreds of thousands of acres starting at the cross of the Tombigbee and Black Warrior Rivers in the central west of the state. The bamboo helped Indians build sturdy waterproof houses, weave resting mats and fine baskets, and make rafts and arrow shafts and canteens and countless other things. Horses and cattle grazed amid the dense cane, and Indians hunted for wild game. Deer and bears and turkeys made homes in the high grass; Indian warriors on the run from federal troops and enslaved people trying to escape their owners later made a hiding place of it. Before European colonists settled in Alabama, its forests were alive with longleaf pine, that skinny gray-black-trunked tree with fuzzy green needles, and weighty American chestnuts. Loblolly pines stretched out near streams and swamps, clean-cut green leaves and short needles all around.

In the eighteenth century, Spanish missionaries made their way up from Florida, the French from Louisiana to the west. From the east came the British, crossing through the Carolinas and Georgia. Upon their arrival, they cleared the canebrakes and cut down the longleaf pine to plant corn and cotton. Farmers then began to replant forests with shortleaf pine; it grew faster. It also became the core of Alabama's timber industry, to be used as pulpwood for making paper and then lumber for construction. These days, that move is now backfiring: the sandy, drought-prone soils of the central region are proving inhospitable to shortleaf pine, as much hotter nights and winters allow insects to crawl through the green for longer periods. Pine beetle outbreaks were at an epidemic level in 2024. The increasing occurrence of thunderstorms and hurricanes in a state used to witnessing them, but not at this climate change–induced scale, knocks down and damages trees that then become nests for the pine beetles. But these are the smaller disasters. The whole picture is that forests are becoming something else entirely: as the temperature rises and rainfall fluctuates, trees will likely start to grow farther apart, to conserve water and better their chances of survival, and sunlight will spread out on the forest floor. Grass will spring high between trees, and trees themselves will likely grow shorter and stouter—forests will become savannas.

Farmers and landowners have been in moments of ecological crisis before—the American chestnut was decimated by a blight in the early twentieth century that killed almost all the mature chestnuts east of the Mississippi—but this crisis feels like something more dangerous. Down in Mobile Bay, a shallow pool of the Gulf, the waters are rising and killing submerged plant life. In this hotter and wetter climate, the islands in Fowl River, in Mobile County, are disappearing. Farmers are feeling the inconsistencies of the rain, too: it is either too much or not enough. Too little rain puts the green under stress, and too much erodes the soil underneath it, leaching its nutrients. With more intense rain comes exceptional drought. Damned if they do, damned if they don't, some might say.

In the Black Belt, which rambles across the state and into Mississippi and Georgia on either side, the black soil once prime for growing cotton is now refusing to absorb the sewage from the houses and trailers of its residents, and more frequent rainfall is turning the situation into another disaster. The way Alabamians think about themselves is due in great part to the environment. All this abundance and its violent settlement—whoever has more force takes the spoils—have bred an entitlement to the land and a defiance to anything that is in the way. The state motto is *Audemus jura nostra defendere*, or "We

Dare Defend Our Rights." Protect the state. Even in its decaying days.

* * *

Alabama Fever began as soon as the Creek War came to a close in 1814. Well, it had already begun, but it officially started once the Indians admitted defeat. The 21 million acres of land the Creek had to turn over to the federal government were now fair game, and white settlers flooded in to lay claim to it. It was almost possible for the settlers to believe that this new terrain was virgin, had been lying in wait for them all along. They saw themselves as pioneers, machetes in hand, whacking down trees, spreading and staking like other settlers throughout the American union. This was the cotton frontier, stretching from Alabama and Mississippi to northern Louisiana, Arkansas, and Texas. Factories around the world needed cotton, and cotton needed people to cultivate and export it. In 1810, Alabama's population was fewer than 10,000 people. Ten years on, it was nearly 130,000. A third of those new arrivals were enslaved Africans. Ten years after that, greatly due to slave owners forcibly breeding those Africans and importing more of them, the population was over 300,000.

In this freewheeling market, the hottest commodities were cotton and enslaved people. The smart settler would sell cotton to buy enslaved people, make more cotton with those additional enslaved people, and, with the spike in profits, keep on buying land to expand and expand. Alabama Fever, then, was not just about fulfilling the prophetic destiny of the American union, pushing out its borders as far as the settlers could see. It was also about trading in bodies to lay the foundations for the twenty-second state, freedom and bondage coexisting until they no longer could. By the 1860s, almost half a million enslaved people resided in Alabama. The outside appetite for cotton was spiraling upward. So the frontier swelled, collapsing more land and bodies in its path to replace soil that was already no good. On the settlers went, in heat, fevered, sometimes feverish. God help what stood in their way.

In elementary school, our teachers had us play *The Oregon Trail* so many afternoons, I lost count. The computer game was supposed to teach children what it was like to be a white male settler with a family in the 1800s, traveling on a two-thousand-mile wagon path known as the Oregon Trail to make a home out west. It paid homage to Alabama's, and America's, pioneer story. After deciding whether to use horses, oxen, or mules, and what kind of wagon and supplies to take, we had to navigate a series of troubles on the way to our new home in Oregon: wagon accidents, blizzards, dysentery. There were Indian characters with feathers and tomahawks, and getting into conflict with them was another way to fail to reach our destination. The Indians could attack our wagons and leave us with nothing. Or they could help guide us across river crossings in exchange for warm clothes. (Neither actually happened in real life with any frequency.) I played the game competitively, waiting for the days our class went to the computer lab after lunch and I could try, my belly full from Sloppy Joes and soda, to beat previous scores. I could imagine being a white man in a wide-brimmed hat, fighting the odds with a musket, emerging victorious. I could almost place myself in the story.

CHAPTER TWO

Indecent Pride

When Alabama went to war from a city that was the original capital of the breakaway nation—Montgomery—under the president of this new Confederacy—Jefferson Davis—it was with the delirious swagger of a place that had gotten away with so much that it had nothing else to fear. But what the Civil War left behind has always been more important to Alabama than what happened during it. The story the state started to tell about itself began in the aftermath. All the ills that remained—poverty, illiteracy, stunted economic development—were due to how northerners had ravaged the South after the fighting was done. Marauders had burned schools and railroads, any important infrastructure they could get their hands on, to destroy this place. Reconstruction only made matters worse. Starting in 1867 and for a decade on, Black Alabamians held political office and made up part of the delegation sent to the first postwar state constitutional convention. Most white Alabamians saw this sudden, swift progress as farce and then complete tragedy. The *Montgomery Advertiser* said around the time, "If the negro must rule Alabama permanently, whether in person or by proxy, the white man must ultimately leave the state."

This was what they had been afraid of. Between eighty and ninety thousand white men from Alabama from the ages of seventeen to forty-five, and some older than that (and some surely younger), enlisted in the Confederate Army. Twenty-three of those boys and men were kin to Lewis Calvin Chappelle IV, or Calvin, as everybody called him. Calvin was born in 1978 in Montgomery, the elder of two. His father, Lewis Calvin Chappelle III, grew up in Mobile, where his own father and most of the rest of the extended family had made the sleepy coastal city their home.

One day in August 1989, Calvin and his younger brother, Will, got up before sunrise and piled into their dad's pickup truck to make the almost four-hour drive south from Montgomery, listening to Jefferson Airplane and the Grateful Dead on the way down. Not too long before, Calvin's father had discovered that they had eight ancestors who had fought at the oranged-brick fortress of Fort Morgan, which was surrounded by white beach and jutted into both the Gulf and Mobile Bay. One was his fourth great-grandfather. During the Civil War, the fort had been the first line of defense for the city of Mobile, until a Union naval and land attack forced Confederate troops to surrender in August 1864. In 1989, the 125th anniversary of the Battle of Mobile Bay, reenactors planned to stage the battle at the fort. The event was the first time Calvin, Will, and their father, who went by "Chip," had ever heard of reenactments. Chip had seen a notice of the event in the newspaper and excitedly made a plan to go watch with his boys.

There was nothing on the final road leading to Fort Morgan except a few condos and beach houses. When the trio arrived, it was dizzyingly hot. The fort was gigantic, glowering under the puffy sky. They had to pass through an arched tunnel to get to the heart of the complex, and Calvin looked at the bleaching walls and green fields in awe: it was a whole lot of space to run around. Several hundred reenactors roamed the interior. The U.S. Army Corps of Engineers had begun construction of Fort Morgan in 1819; enslaved people built it with their bare hands using brick, mortar, sandstone, granite, iron, and cement. Their blood was under the earth of all the reenactments Calvin, Will, and Chip would come to attend.

Calvin was eleven and too young to carry a rifle, but he could take on the role of a wartime musician. He began to learn how to play the drum and the fife, a skinny flutelike instrument. There were very few drummers and fifers in the Deep South, he was told, much less child musicians. "Everybody loved us because we were the field music. It made it special for other people," he recalled. "People would say, 'There are the Chappelle boys.'" Their drum instructor was a retired army musician who would later take Calvin and Will to high schools to give demonstrations on the music of the period. Most reenactments in the late 1980s and early '90s happened around the anniversary cycle, and Calvin, Will, and Chip went from the 125th celebration of one battle to the 130th commemoration of another. These kinds of big gatherings would never happen again; by the time the 150th anniversary reenactments took place, attendance had dropped. Spectators would not have the same interest in them when they could go on the internet to learn about the battles instead. Calvin and his brother and their dad joined the Thirty-Third Alabama Infantry Regiment, a reenactment unit supportive of his music. (Calvin was the "rock star" of the reenacting scene, he joked.) The men appreciated him, and he never had to march in drills or clean weapons. He got to stand out.

About a decade before Fort Morgan, Chip had come to the capital to attend a small liberal arts school called Huntingdon College, near Alabama State, where my parents met. He didn't graduate until years later—he had Calvin when he was eighteen and had to leave school and pick up paying work—but he found other ways to indulge his obsession with history. Because Chip's own father had been away working for much of his childhood, his grandparents and uncles took Chip close and raised him and told him stories about what kind of people they came from. That they descended from a certain kind of stock: men who had worked hard for their families without relying on anybody else, risked their lives to see the world outside Alabama, helped make the state what it had become. These were stories of courage and sacrifice, stories told to enthrall a boy and make him proud. It was because of the elders in Chip's life—Calvin used the word *elders*—that he could understand that the past was present, meant everything to how a person should be. There exists a photo of Calvin's namesake, his great-grandfather Lewis Calvin Chappelle, holding him when he was an infant. His father and grandfather are in the photo, too, four generations in one place.

I met Calvin, as these things tend to happen, in a roundabout sort of way. I knew I wanted to get to know someone who was passionate about the Confederate legacy that haunted and moved Alabama and who had a personal connection to it. And I wanted to have thoughtful conversations with that person about the Civil War, about slavery and race, and about our home state, reflecting on matters both emotional and intellectual. I half-heartedly reached out on Facebook to a few people I had met at an event for a Confederate memorial, but nothing materialized. I next thought about Confederate Memorial Park, a state-run museum I knew little about and had never visited. Six hundred thousand dollars of the annual state budget went to funding the park, and that funding was growing more controversial as time passed. Once a home for poor and sick Confederate veterans, it is now a museum and library; three hundred soldiers are buried there. Admission is free, and tours cost four dollars for adults—unless you are a senior or a veteran, when it is three—and one dollar for kids under eighteen. A state congressman from Huntsville had proposed in 2020 that tax money stop being spent to operate the place; there were much better places for the dollars to go, he thought, than to one that brought so much pain to Black Alabamians.

I was a little uneasy setting out from my parents' house the morning Calvin and I met, unsure of how welcoming the museum would be to a curious Black Alabamian. When I arrived at the park, about thirty miles north of Montgomery in a township called Mountain Creek, a metal sign curved over the road greeted me, a Confederate flag blowing in the sky on either side. At the turnoff on U.S. Route 31, another Confederate flag waved from a pole in the far distance, the park's calling card. When I entered the carpeted, shoebox-size museum, which felt like the outdated living room of an aging relative, Calvin, the museum's director, immediately came up to greet me from the front desk. He was courteous and also curious. (I got the sense he didn't usually receive visitors who looked like me.) When I told him the kind of person I was looking to talk to, he looked at me for a minute, thinking. He smiled and nodded. Then he volunteered himself. I would come to see that he has an unrelenting pride in his story, the kind of pride that had named him the fourth Lewis Calvin Chappelle in his family. The kind of pride that still revered the indecency of his elders. On the days we met, usually with someone from the Alabama Historical Commission, I noticed the huge dark beard grazing his collar bone, his old-fashioned-seeming reading spectacles, and how he spoke with a deliberateness that let me know he would always be cautious with me, regardless of how eager he was to talk. We felt worlds apart, but we kept trying to connect, because that's what you do down here; it's only polite.

Not every white Alabamian wanted secession—we know only that 61 percent of delegates at the Alabama Secession Convention, most of whom had large slaveholdings, did—but when the Confederacy started drafting troops in 1862, boys and men would have looked bad to their communities if they did not sign up, Calvin said. His ancestors had thought and done things that Calvin would not think or do now, but he still felt a reverence for them: "They came before me. They dealt with things as they felt was appropriate, as best they could. I don't know what they were going through, and I'm sure their lives were a lot more difficult than mine." And so he thought soldiers who did own enslaved people and went to war to defend that practice should also be commemorated. "We commemorate that the country was divided, that it went to war, and it started the long process of trying to heal. We're looking at where our nation was, where it is today," he said. The last thing he wanted to do was judge them. "We all know that slavery was wrong. We all know the reasons why slavery was wrong. We can't talk about the good ol' days, because they weren't really the good ol' days. But look at nineteenth-century Americans as a whole, whether in the North or South. Most white individuals did have some racial tendencies. It was part of what they were born into, it was part of the culture, it was part of what they were surrounded by every single day," he said, taking time to locate his words. "So how can you judge the past by today's moral standards? I don't think most historians judge in that way. We learn from our mistakes."

I said that the moral standard then did include people who thought slavery was wrong, even in our home state.

He didn't disagree. "It was frowned upon by some, but probably not the vast majority of the South," he said.

One day at Confederate Memorial Park, I pressed Calvin on the question of moral standards; a journalist who had recently come to the museum later wrote an article about how it kept running because of the more than half a million dollars in state funds. Meanwhile, Black spaces like the Safe House Black History Museum in Greensboro, which told a story of rural civil rights activism, fought to stay open. The reporter wrote that Confederate Memorial Park wanted to tell a history of the Civil War, but put "impartial" in scare quotes. The article was not wrong about the numbers. Calvin told me he had been feeling anxious about talking lately, wondering if I would accurately represent his views without politicizing them. He brought up the northern Alabamians who had opposed war, who couldn't identify with the planters, and whose livelihoods didn't depend on the plantation economy of their more southern neighbors. In their resistance was a practicality about their interests; nothing was pure. "There were men in north Alabama who were against secession, or may have said, 'Let the planters fight their war.' They didn't want to have anything to do with it," he said. "It wasn't driven by slavery. There may have been some who were against the institution, but they had no stock in it." Calvin excused himself to check a family in to the museum. He was the only one working the desk that day.

Calvin recognized, couldn't deny, that slavery was at the root of the war, but he wouldn't criticize the Confederacy. "You can look back at the writings. Both sides thought they were doing the right thing, both sides thought that they were doing what their forefathers would have wanted them to do," he said. "Both thought that they were citizens of the United States—even though the Confederacy is an entirely different government, right—but they all felt that they were Americans doing the right thing."

A quarter, maybe a third, of the men who left Alabama for the war never came back. They died from disease and infection and wounds during battle. There were slave owners in the mix; after all, it was a rich man's war, as Calvin called it. And there were more who had never enslaved people, but who still fought for their state and their race and the preservation of both. For these fighters, the alternative—an economic alliance with Black laborers against the white planter class—was unacceptable compared to the dream of becoming part of the planters' ranks. When the surviving soldiers returned home, they found white Alabama demoralized and broken. The old way of life was gone, and their world was about to transform. "The South really had a hard time recovering after the war because such a large portion of the male population was gone," Calvin said. The white male population, that is. White women of means had to make do for themselves for the first time ever, taking up the tasks of their dead husbands and brothers and sons when it came to managing the home and business.

First came the mourning and the reburying of the dead, at least of the bodies they could recover. Ladies' memorial associations raised money for gravestones and took care of the maimed and the depressed, the widows and the orphans. The women would also take up the task of honoring their dead. Right away, a narrative had to be forged, a story to protect the memories of their loved ones; the losers had to pass something on. Confederate veterans began having reunions, commemorations of brethren who had passed. "It would be very hard to ask a society to put things aside like that and forget," Calvin told me. "Had the North lost, would they not have wanted to do the same thing?" But instead of a story that included accountability or remorse, an investigation into why their fight was doomed from the start, the survivors decided to remember selectively and to invent. For white Alabamians, the mission was simple.

In 1894, nearly thirty years after the war, white women throughout the Deep South on a similar mission started up a federation of Confederate women's organizations, a "sisterhood," as a founding member called it, eventually to be named the United Daughters of the Confederacy. Unofficial chapters with the same name had already sprouted up around the region. Anna Davenport Raines, from Savannah, Georgia, the daughter of a Confederate officer, wrote to a Caroline Meriwether Goodlett in Nashville, Tennessee, about merging their work for veterans; both women had been involved in veteran mutual aid and memorial associations in their respective towns. Their friends and neighbors and relatives signed up for the UDC in droves—thirty thousand of them by 1902. Beyond tending to the graves of fallen soldiers and erecting monuments in their honor, the women involved themselves in the business of education. For UDC members in Alabama, it would be the most important and efficient way to pass on "memories of the South" and of the Confederacy to young people in the state, as Caroline Janney writes in *Remembering the Civil War: Reunion and the Limits of Reconciliation*. (White young people, to be specific; they were the only ones allowed to attend public school.)

The ladies would have to use their "might," Raines wrote to Goodlett, to shield children from the "falsehoods" about the Civil War in school textbooks—details that associated, even loosely, the antebellum planter class in Alabama and other states with slavery or racism or grotesque violence. Or with being on the wrong side, rightful losers in a war of decency and humanity. The seeds of the "Lost Cause" would be dug into the soil of this battleground; the actual gunfight had been surrendered, but there were other clashes to be won. The prize would be a pristine history, carefully culled by a ladies' society preoccupied with race and class, so that the women they knew could maintain a connection to the old order of living and their privileged beginnings. It would become a project around which many wives, daughters, sisters, and mothers of veterans would rally, and then with which they would become obsessed. They would not let the victors write their story, they decided. They would tell it themselves.

* * *

Which is how we got into this mess. The two public stories of Alabama that its historical commission has forced to recline intimately together are of Confederate nostalgia and civil rights redemption. From secession and war to nonviolent protest and reconciliation in one easy, straight line. The ugliness of what came before both—Indian removal, the slave trade, Reconstruction, and Jim Crow—is mostly absent. The time between the end of the Creek War and the start of the Civil War appears like a faded cut, a flesh-colored bruise, less than five decades of extermination and brutality and riches and decadence almost not there. By the 1860s, Montgomery had more depots to hold enslaved people than churches or schools. But it took until 2013 for there to be commemorative markers placed around Commerce Street, where the enslaved got off boats at one end, on the cloudy indigos of the Alabama River. They were chained together and marched to auctions held in Court Square. A parade of the doomed. A cast-iron fountain, lifting crumbling statues of minor Greek gods, now stands in the square. The marker there, put up in 2002, states that the ground underneath is where "slaves of all ages were auctioned, along with land and livestock, standing in a line to be inspected."

A marker also went up at Union Station downtown, right near the lash of the Alabama River known as Gun Island Chute, that explains how slave traders regularly shipped enslaved bodies on train cars that went through the stop. The station is still Richardsonian Romanesque with red brick, black roofs, grandly arched windows, and thick columns, backing up to the water. Another marker went up at the office of the Equal Justice Initiative (EJI), which has defended death-row inmates in Alabama for three decades and made its home in a former warehouse that kept enslaved people. The last marker was posted at the intersection of Monroe and Lawrence Streets and references slave depots over on Dexter Avenue. As the EJI was applying for approval to add all these markers to the downtown narrative, it faced resistance. The then mayor, a conservative politician named Todd Strange, said he was uncomfortable with the idea; the city already had a plaque addressing slavery, on the Court Square fountain, which he thought was enough. But he eventually agreed because he thought the project would boost tourism. Strange said he came around because "part of the reason we were interested in these markers is because we have dozens on the Civil War experience and many about the civil rights movement. But we don't have many about slavery."

Five years after that, the EJI put up something more imposing, a structure that would dominate that crowded historical grid: a memorial devoted to the victims of lynching. The markers had hinted at the racial terror that had built the city; the memorial put it in plain view. I had gone to most of the city's civil rights museums on school field trips as a kid, and when I went to the memorial on assignment for the *New Yorker* as an adult, I suddenly felt I knew nothing about my state's history. I had been taught very little about lynching in school and had no idea that it happened in this country with such frequency that, as the EJI has documented, more than 4,440 Black people were lynched across twenty states from 1877 to 1950, Reconstruction and the civil rights movement on either end. The memorial is devoted to murder victims, some whose identities are still unknown, from 805 counties. Nearly all the counties are in the South.

It was pouring rain when I first visited. I parked in front of the EJI office and pulled up my trousers to avoid getting them soaked as I ran into the building next door. The EJI had built a small museum to give historical context to the memorial. Inside were videos and holograms and interactive displays on how the business of slavery evolved into the business of mass incarceration, and how a brutally unequal criminal justice system helped that metamorphosis along. I looked at a photo of a crowd of white townspeople watching a lynching with their children, wearing their Sunday finest and posing for photos and eating snacks and drinking soda and lemonade. I looked at jars of soil, crimson reds and tangerine oranges and powdery browns and blacks, taken from the earth beneath trees where people had been lynched. On each jar was the name of the victim and the date and county of their death. A staff member came to get me from the exhibit, and then we walked to the memorial.

From down the street, the structure looked almost serene, an architectural feat of 805 steel monuments geometrically arranged on a grassy hill. As I entered the dark space, surrounded by what I could now see were heavy and rusting columns, each imprinted with the names of victims under the county where their murders took place, that serenity mutated into dread. I navigated around several of the columns until the ground gave way, sloping down so that the monuments were now suspended above me, evoking lifeless bodies hanging from trees. I realized later that the monuments also resembled coffins, in a way. My dread slipped into a feeling that resembled awe. There were no other sounds apart from dripping water: a light waterfall covered one of the memorial walls. The sky was darkening. I was alone. I stood for a few minutes reading plaques that detailed the circumstances of some of the murders, and then took out my phone and started typing. Caleb Gadly, lynched in 1894 for walking behind the wife of the white man for whom he worked. David Walker, accused of using inappropriate language with a white woman in 1908; a mob hanged him and his wife and their four children. Ballie Crutchfield, lynched in 1901 by a mob searching for her brother; when they could not find him, they decided she would do.

Outside, on the smooth pavement and wide sidewalks, the story is dense but orderly. Visitors can draw simple and clean connections between the terrors of the past and the glory that later came from surviving those pains—the elegance of suffering and loss and eventual triumph, all part of growing up. At the end of this tale is what can now be seen when looking around: integrated offices and restaurants and bars filled with conversation and laughter. We come together over soul food and beer. But the uncertain light of the memorial had obliterated any neat ending, made clear it had not been earned. The space began to seem otherworldly because of this, and disorienting. I walked outside. It had stopped raining, but the landscape was coated with gray and swollen clouds still hovered above my head. Duplicates of each column inside were laid out on the cropped stiff grass at the edges of the memorial. The intent was for officials or community leaders from each county named on the columns to come and claim their statue. They could then display it as an addition to their own public stories. Many of their historical grounds look as conflicted and incomplete as ours.

The *Montgomery Advertiser* is nearby, walking distance from the Hank Williams statue and museum, the hickory-fire ribs and pulled pork at Dreamland Bar-B-Que, the bus stop where Rosa Parks used to wait for her ride to work, and more churches than should be within a square mile. My dad, who taught journalism, had done some writing for the newspaper and had once taken me at a young age, awestruck, to meet editors there. Around the time the memorial opened, the paper began a series examining its coverage of hundreds of cases of lynching. Its first installment discovered that the newspaper often engaged in empty moralizing about the violence and justified the targeting of Black Alabamians. "All right-thinking people deplore lynchings," one editorial began with a gentle and reasonable appeal to its white readers. "But it is wise to utter a solemn truth, with the old, old lemon brought home again, as long as there are attempts at rape by Black men, red men or yellow men on white women there will be lynchings." The editorial was written in 1919—not so long ago. It is a source of simultaneous pride and pain that progress in Alabama during the century since has usually been the result of a ferocious push and pull among competing visions of the state. But there are visions of ourselves that need to be discarded: as a place that ended state-sanctioned terrorism once the Emancipation Proclamation was issued, as a place that is willing to look its crimes in the face. The state has the lack of the latter trait in common with the country at large. Things just tend to look more obvious down here.

CHAPTER THREE

The Same Dream

My family lived in South Montgomery in the 1990s, a decade after Calvin was on the west side, the oldest section of Alabama's capital. He grew up near Montgomery Mall, which was where my mom loved to shop. He and his friends wandered their mostly white, middle-class neighborhood and went over to the mall. "We were free-ranged," he recalled. "Today you couldn't get away with that stuff; parents would get in trouble." When it got dark out, they went home; that was about the only rule he abided. Neighborhoods in West and South Montgomery, by the time I lived there, were rarely both white and middle class. It was hard to imagine what life had been like before these parts of town became the Black sides—well, the proof was still there: the older handsomely framed houses, the newer suburban cutout homes built with another kind of resident in mind. But everything else—the darker occupants, the increased poverty, the higher incidence of crime, the public schools where kids scored too low on their standardized tests—had changed. From the second we moved in, my parents were itching to get out. They had no plans to send me to the school for which I was zoned.

Calvin had no problem going to his, which was Bear Elementary, with white and Black kids, and then Cloverdale Junior High, where he remembered white students being in the minority. Class and race worked in my hometown like they did in most other places: it said something if a white person lived on the west or south sides when I was growing up, or in central Montgomery if it wasn't in the elegant confines of Old Cloverdale and other historic neighborhoods, because it usually signified that they didn't have the means to get out with their white neighbors who had left the area. It meant their kids might have to go to schools that were not as well funded or high achieving. It also meant that when my family moved to a pleasant neighborhood on the south side, my parents tried to get me into a school in another part of town as fast as they could. There was still a busing program in the 1990s, a remnant of the public school desegregation efforts of the 1950s and '60s that aimed to put just enough Black students into white schools to satisfy the law. My dad applied for the program, and I got placed in an elementary school on the east side in time for my first school year in Alabama. But my parents drove me there every morning and picked me up every afternoon, for my comfort, instead of letting me take the bus after a boy elbowed me the first time I rode it. I didn't realize until I was older that kids were supposed to go to schools located near them, so they could walk or bike or at least take a short bus ride there. Much of my childhood was spent in the back seat of my dad's car, being taken to and from school, as he maneuvered around classes he was teaching at Alabama State, clear across town, and ducked out of staff meetings and office hours to come get my brothers and me. It was a mixture of extreme protectiveness and self-sacrifice I could barely appreciate then.

After an unreasonably big breakfast every day of scrambled eggs, bacon or sausage, and toaster waffles—my parents seemed to think we would die of malnutrition otherwise—my dad took my eldest younger brother and me to our respective schools on the east side and then went to the university where he had met my mom and now worked as a professor. The campus sprawled across downtown. My mother helped out when she could between nursing school classes and then night shifts at a hospital after she graduated. An aspiration my parents shared, which I then adopted, was to move east. Moving would manifest our Alabama dream—a comfortable home, a thriving family—and be proof that we had made it, in a bigger and languid stucco house with fuzzy, bright front and back lawns on a cul-de-sac in a gated, or at least exclusive, subdivision. Most of our neighbors would be white, and our zoned schools would be among the best in the county. For a while, even, I lied to a friend in middle school, saying I lived in her neighborhood, a subdivision called Arrowhead, ready to try on what it sounded like, until she found me out. When we did actually move to Arrowhead while I was in high school, a neighborhood with a name that vaguely evoked its Creek beginnings and where the loudest sounds came from birds in the window-dusting trees and from rotating sprinklers, more than a few of our neighbors would also be Black. It turned out a lot of us had the same dream.

* * *

With the end of the Civil War in 1865 came an opening, not big enough for an entire people, but adequate room to let some pass. Black Alabamians saw their chance to join the theater of real living. They aspired to do things like go to the polls, under federal protection, and elect people who looked like them, experienced life like them. They had to. All around them was obscene violence: white people shooting, drowning, and torturing former slaves, even tricking them with promises of new jobs and instead selling them as slaves to Brazil and Cuba, cheating them out of their earnings and extorting them.

Voting had an outsize role in the priorities and needs of Black Alabamians after emancipation because, along with the need to work for pay and without abuses, much of what they wanted was space of their own and the means to keep it. The surest way to acquire and keep land was casting a ballot and being fairly represented in the local courts and legislature, at polling offices, and on county commissions. Their efforts were doomed: the violent confinement and constant surveillance of their lives under slavery would seamlessly extend to what was supposed to be freedom. Alabama, like the rest of the Deep South, ensured this. But until that extension was complete, voting stood for a lot of things. It meant the ability to participate, to choose, to be counted. After being told for so long what to do, where to live, when to work, and how to be, Black folks would decide for themselves. On Election Day in 1874, in the city of Mobile, some of the last of the 110 West Africans kidnapped, enslaved, and brought to Alabama woke up and went out to vote. Oluale Kossola, who would become a kind of leader of Africatown, the community they created by necessity, and who would decide to go by the name "Cudjo Lewis," visited the nearest polls with other survivors only fourteen years after they had first arrived on the Mobile River. The man who stopped them from voting that day, Tim Meaher, was the same one who had enslaved them on his riverside plantation—he told election officials that the group was not "of this country"—but Kossola and the others went to another polling place and cast their votes there as Alabamians.

From the late 1860s on, Black men won office in the U.S. Senate; they also became mayors and sheriffs and postmasters and local representatives across the Deep South. Just a few years before, they had been enslaved. Now, as elected officials, they were scaring some white people and seducing the convictions of others. Pinckney Benton Stewart Pinchback was briefly the first Black governor of Louisiana—and of any state—and Robert Smalls was a congressman from South Carolina; both had white supporters. Several formerly enslaved men, like Jeremiah Haralson and Benjamin Turner, represented Alabama in the U.S. House of Representatives; James Rapier, born free and a prosperous planter, joined them. Dozens of Black representatives were elected to the Alabama state legislature, where they helped build the public education system. Haralson, who was enslaved as a child, helped

Turner with his congressional campaign and then became a state legislator. He was a U.S. congressman at age twenty-eight. From Selma (though born in Muscogee County, Georgia), Turner taught himself to read and write. Frederick Douglass heard Haralson speak in New Orleans in 1872 and wrote that he was "one of the most amusing, ready, witted, and gifted debaters that took part in the proceedings." Then president Ulysses S. Grant consulted with him on federal appointments in Alabama.

Violence was still everywhere. In the year leading up to the retaking of the governorship by Alabama Democrats in 1870, Black and white Republicans and their supporters were murdered and attacked. The Black politicians did not have it easy, were challenged at all corners. Reconstruction also came and went before any of the Black residents of Lowndes County, in the heart of the Black Belt, could take a minute to dwell in it. In 1874, twelve hundred Black people in the Black Belt town of Eufaula could and did vote for the Republican Party candidates. Two years on, in the presidential election, only ten could. In February 1877, Haralson would testify before a Senate subcommittee about the fraud that had prevented his reelection. The majority of the committee agreed the race had been fraudulent, but they refused to unseat his opponent. Haralson was the last Black man elected to Congress from Alabama until 1992. He and his peers saw less than a decade of whiplash political freedom.

The Compromise of 1877 allowed Republicans to keep the presidency after the disputed election the year before, but it granted the Democratic Party's wish to see the last federal troops withdrawn from the South. The Democrats could firmly regain power in Alabama. It took not long after that for Lowndes County to earn its nickname, "Bloody Lowndes," for the terror that came next. The county's Black population was ten times the size of its white one, and white residents did whatever possible to maintain power, from enacting Black Codes that controlled how far and to where their Black neighbors could travel, for whom they could work, whom they could marry, and how they could behave, to a sustained siege of murders, attacks, and evictions. When Jim Crow legislation passed in 1891, putting segregation into law, the story of Alabama was already flattening Reconstruction into oblivion.

As their white neighbors watched, the newly free tried to experiment in living. They went to the courthouse to register as voters, roamed the state to pursue work that interested them, and acquired homes. They had what W. E. B. Du Bois called "land hunger," saving money for even mediocre plots nobody else wanted, as long as white landowners or the government would sell to them. They were threatened for their voting efforts, chased off their land—many a lynching came about because white people wanted their victims' property—arrested for vagrancy, and made convict laborers when they tried to leave the surroundings of their former plantations for something different. Besides forcing the Black free into penal slavery if they tried to stop working for their former masters, the Black Codes meant they could not own arms or testify in court on the same footing as white people, and could see their children sold into indentured servitude if the state saw fit to do so. Once Reconstruction ended, and the political power of Black men was taken away just as quickly, though more brutally, as it had been given, certain white women in Alabama used the resulting opening for their own ends. Their efforts to commemorate and memorialize white Confederate veterans through the United Daughters of the Confederacy not only gave them control of the state's story, but kept the racial order culturally intact, too.

Everyone had to contend with the wreckage, but the newly free waited in vain for relief. The Black Belt was still the domain of the rural white elite, who had a disproportionate share of political power in the state. Despite there being only a couple thousand active voters in some counties, the area possessed more representatives than most other regions. To avoid muddying the color line, its officials put a chokehold on progressive policy, like public health, education, and infrastructure programs that would have helped both Black and white residents. Former governor George Wallace's "standing in the schoolhouse door" meant that he encouraged white-only private schools in the late 1960s and '70s while bragging about Alabama "having the lowest property taxes of probably any state"— a distinction that deprived Black and white students in public schools. Maintain the racial order at all costs. In the 1930s, Alabama received New Deal payments from the federal government that would have helped intensely struggling Black farmers, but it denied them the same loans given to white farmers and overtaxed their land, leading to their evictions and foreclosures. This was not any kind of freedom Black Alabamians had heard of or seen before.

* * *

Indian removal and the domestic slave trade, known as the Second Middle Passage, are intimately linked. Settlers had to force the Indians out to make way for the enslaved; it was a matter of space. Traders moved enslaved people—first by foot, later on steamboat and trains—from Upper South states like Tennessee and Virginia on down to New Orleans and Natchez, Mississippi's busiest slave-trading city, to be sold in places like Alabama. More than half the sold people had been stolen from parents, children, spouses.

Coming the other way were the Creek. Most Creek families who survived the Creek War were forced to migrate out of Alabama, captured and removed. An exodus of Indian bodies. "U.S. soldiers built stockades to house the Creeks until they could get them moving," Lou Vickery writes in *The Rise of the Poarch Band of Creek Indians*, quoting historian A. J. Pemberton. "All over Creek country the soldiers went, bringing in the old and young, male and female and their babes, the sick, the lame, and the immobilized."

Many Creek resisted, refusing the money and the autonomy the federal government promised if they made the journey voluntarily, but it made no difference. "The soldiers hunted them down like hunting wild beasts and when they found them, drove them under threats and blows like cattle to these stockades," Vickery quotes. "These stockades were over-crowded, disease broke out among them and many of them died with dysentery. Poor food and poor water, no doctors and no medicine."

From the stockades, soldiers packed Creek families tightly onto barges that steamboats pulled down the Alabama River to Mobile during the hot summer, usually moving on to Mississippi and then down the Gulf Coast to New Orleans. Disembarking months after their journey began, the Creek then faced all that lay before them: a cold wasteland of wilderness stretching to Oklahoma through which they would have to march, prey to both animal and human predators.

The last enslaved Africans who were compelled to migrate to Alabama some thirty years later had to be captured and removed. A journey of Black bodies. Along with a host of others taken as captives in West Africa, to be turned over to William Foster on the *Clotilda*, Oluale Kossola was "yoked by forked sticks and tied in a chain," as Zora Neale Hurston writes, then marched to the stockades. "After three days, they were incarcerated in the barracoons [stockades] at Ouidah, near the Bight of Benin. During the weeks of his existence in the barracoons, Kossola was bewildered and anxious about his fate. Before him was a thundering and crashing ocean that he had never seen before. Behind him was everything that he called home. There in the barracoon, as there in his Alabama home, Kossola was transfixed between two worlds, fully belonging to neither."

According to standard definition, stockades are traditionally used as a means of defense in battle, a barrier from attack. Or as a prison, a place to keep criminals. Their third use, as a way station for the trafficking of dark bodies, has never been acknowledged.

* * *

The Black Belt once had the richest cotton soil in the state. In 1860, Dallas County was ahead of all the others in cotton production, slaveholding, and per capita wealth. During the Civil War, the county's graceful and haughty capital, Selma, became an arsenal and manufacturing center. Nathan Bedford Forrest, Confederate general and later Ku Klux Klan grand wizard, staged his last stand to save the Confederacy there as the war wound to its end. He conceded defeat as the arsenal burned. Union soldiers set fire to what else they could and moved on to Montgomery. Seven days later, when the South surrendered on April 9, 1865, Black and white Alabamians suddenly found themselves in "dark and doubtful days," as Abraham Lincoln said, looking for a new way to coexist.

"They were rebuilding their state," Calvin said of Alabamians after the war. Some more than others: formerly enslaved Black people moved on to work as sharecroppers and tenant farmers, and they began to put the landscape back together. As had been the way for more than two hundred years, Black laborers would do much of the building and take on much of the risk. Even the few Black Alabamians who acquired farms, or any land of their own, would rarely be free to enjoy it in peace.

Like the family of Mary McDonald. One night in September 1965, when Mary was three and a half, night riders came to her house in Lowndes County and shot inside. The bullets hit the bed of Mary's baby brother Walter, who had Down syndrome, and shattered the window above his crib. The family thanks God that Mary's older sister Flora had gotten up to get Walter and take him to sleep in her bed. As soon as they laid back down, they heard the shots. Bullets also tore through the walls of the house, trespassing the bedroom shared by Mary's parents, Pattie Mae and Leon Sr.

At that time, "whites relied primarily on economic reprisals and verbal harassment, and they operated mainly during daylight," as Hasan Kwame Jeffries writes in *Bloody Lowndes: Civil Rights and Black Power in Alabama's Black Belt*. This nighttime attack was something new. Young civil rights activists who lived in the community converged on Mary's house as soon as they heard the news. They sat under the fruit trees in the yard, consoling the family. Agents from the Federal Bureau of Investigation arrived at the house some hours after the shooting; the local police did not show up until the evening.

Mary's parents had named her after both her grandmothers and her great-grandmother, and she grew up on the land to which her family had held a handwritten deed since 1869. That deed had come to mean many things to her family, one of the most important being the security it gave them. As Mary said, "It's why we were one of the few families in this particular area of Lowndes County that white people could not put off their property." They did try.

It was the Klan, but not entirely so. Small business owners, teachers, law enforcement, husbands, wives, and parents also joined in. "They would ring up your food in the general store in the daytime and put on their white hoods at night," Mary said. She would find out when she was older that the man who ran the nearby general store was a Klansman; his son had played with her brother.

Whenever civil rights activists came to her home and swept the children out of the yard and into the house, Mary knew something was happening. She was nearly the youngest, the second-to-last of ten brothers and sisters and only a few years old, but she knew their visitors were working on something important. Activists had also been gathering at the small two-room building Mary's parents owned down the road from their house, which members of the Student Nonviolent Coordinating Committee used as a library. On so many days after going door-to-door canvassing and registering voters, the young workers would meet at the house to rest, wash, drink, and eat; Pattie cooked for them. Stokely Carmichael gave Mary and her siblings an Etch A Sketch that they fought over to draw on.

Mary was born two years into the 1960s, but it seemed like she had always been grown. She was a prayed-for child, and so were most of her siblings. Pattie's first two children were girls, and then she asked the Lord for a boy, one who would be an overseer for the family. God gave her five sons in a row. Then she prayed for a child who would remind her of herself; Mary's older sister Shirley Ann was born. Pattie and Shirley were almost too alike. They were so stubborn that it was hard for them to get along. Couldn't tell them nothing.

Next, Pattie asked for a child who would remind her of her mother. That was Mary. She was the exact copy of her grandmother. When Mary was a girl and Pattie called her over to rub her back after a long day, Pattie said that even Mary's hands reminded her of her mother's hands. Everywhere Shirley went, people asked her if she was Pattie's daughter; the resemblance was so strong. Shirley would nod and look at her sister Mary and say, "Yes, ma'am. She is, too." So, for a long time, Mary's name was "She is, too."

Mary's mother was fair-skinned and lovely, but tough. Pattie had nerve. She churned her own butter, pasteurized her own milk, and raised hogs, and the family ate better than anybody around. She was self-educated, liked to read, and helped raise more money in church than the other parishioners. It made sense that she was drafted into the civil rights fight, that she offered her house as a shelter for the movement.

Mary has mirthful, kind eyes and extravagantly dark skin. I met her during one of her later lives, as an accidental activist, when I was reporting on a sanitation and environmental crisis in the Black Belt starting in 2018. I was spending time in her town interviewing residents about their septic tanks, which, due to inadequate engineering and climate change, were often contaminating their homes and affecting their health. When we met, I could tell she was observing me, taking me in. Deciding what kind of person I was and if she could trust me. Something I could imagine she had been doing since she was a girl. I didn't know if Mary would trust me as soon as she did. I was a Black person from Alabama, but it had been a long time since I had really been here and known what it was about. I was always getting on a flight back to New York. When I asked to keep in touch, Mary noncommittally gave me her phone number and said she was sure there were other people who would be better to talk to. I called her several months later and asked if she remembered me despite our brief meeting. She did.

We talked about the Belt and its history of activism, and we talked about our respective parents and how they had made this strange place home. When I got to her house, she welcomed me like a cousin who was visiting after an extended spell out of town, where I had forgotten how to take it easy. She served me something to drink, apologized for not cooking.

Mary was a precocious girl. Her mother put her in school a year early, when she was only four, before pre-kindergarten existed in the area, because she used to cry when her older brothers and sisters went off to school. And when Mary went down the road every morning to go to Head Start, she would run all the way back if she forgot to kiss Pattie and tell her she loved her. One day, while she was doing just that, her father told Pattie, "That's going to be the one that takes care of you when you get older." The family believed that Leon Sr., who went by "Bigg," prophesied Mary's future through speaking those words. "He locked me down here," Mary said. She paused for a minute: "Well, I don't want to use those words, 'locked me down.'" A doctor of Pattie's who was fond of Mary said the same thing: no matter where Mary went in the world, she would end up back in this place.

Pattie and Bigg's hosting activists in their home and fostering the library carried enough risk to scare many sensible people out of the local Black freedom movement, yet Mary's parents refused to show fear. But in getting involved, the couple became a new target of the terrorists who lived among them. In the warm months of 1965, before the siege on their house, the family began receiving calls from people telling them to drop the civil rights mess—voices identifying themselves only as the Klan. Then acquaintances who worked as maids and cooks for white families showed up with warnings that they had heard hints of an assassination plot against Bigg. Two white men already watched him every morning as he caught his ride to work and then returned home in the evening. Later on, in August, Pattie and Leon noticed white men, could have been the same ones, staking out the library. Pattie wrote to the Alabama project director for SNCC, warning him and the field secretary for the county seat of Hayneville to stay away from her home, for their own safety. Things were "hot," she wrote. She admitted it was no way to live, but she was going to keep her family put. Their land and house were a kind of freedom not many Black families had.

The McDonald family looked like a genetic mosaic of Black Alabama: Mary's maternal grandmother had Native American in her blood, one of her great-grandfathers was white, and various relatives had pale hair, light eyes, and tawny and reddish and black skin. Pattie protected her own, her elderly parents and her kids, along with the young people in the movement. She hated any man she thought to be cowardly and admired the Black men she and Bigg knew who stood up for their families. The couple had a friend, named JC Coleman Sr., who openly carried his guns where everyone could see them. White men drove around town and in the country in pickup trucks with rifles propped up prominently in the cabs, so he did, too. Those white men told him to take down the guns in his cab, but he refused. When Black residents tried to register to vote in 1965 and their white landowners evicted hundreds of them in retaliation, Pattie's community erected tents on a Black-owned open field to house the refugees. JC volunteered to be one of the security guards protecting the camp. When night riders drove by and shot their guns, JC shot back at them, unfazed.

Bigg got too lit on the weekends, but he looked out for the family, always keeping a .45 pistol on him. He had a day job working for a construction company that laid telephone cables. Bigg had only a third-grade education and still made it to foreman, though he passed out checks for salaries higher than his own to the white people junior to him. He also once farmed; he plowed by moonlight.

The family lived in Hayneville, a town of antebellum and shotgun houses and bawling moss. It is practically overrun by its green, alive and crawling over its serene roads and buildings. Mary's house had six rooms and a covered front porch that faced south. In 1969, Mary's parents added on a storage space, a back porch, and a laundry room. There was something glorious about having space that was all their own, their grassy moat and the towering trees leaping from it. There was a weeping willow tree out in the front yard, with limbs that splayed every which way, shading whatever was underneath. "You could just sit up under that tree, and it was like a tent for you," Mary said. "It was so tall, people used to find our house from the crossroads just by following the top of that tree." (Until lightning hit when she was in her early twenties. "God killed it," she added with a laugh.)

Before the tree fell, Mary and her siblings played a game they called Skinny Cat, where they jumped onto the picnic table under the tree, grabbed a branch, hooked their knees over the branch, and then pulled up their feet and dropped their hands to swing in the air. No one ever forgot the time a six- or seven-year-old Mary went to do the Skinny Cat with hands greasy from fried chicken and slipped straight down, landing on the ground with no breath left in her. No one forgot, but the family called Mary, especially, the historian: she had a pristine memory for vital and not-so-vital dates and happenings. Remembering, to her, was preservation. The surest way for the family to hold on to what was theirs.

In 1970, when Mary was eight, Lowndes County elected its first Black sheriff, and armed black men were on guard as two thousand people gathered to see him sworn in. Mary attended an all-Black school because white and Black kids never went to school together in Lowndes County. After the new sheriff's swearing-in, white people broke into her school. They threw eggs and smeared the walls with marker: "We hate your colored lawman." Mary felt strange that day—not fear, but an ache at the word *hate* on the wall and the reference to her color. It seemed to be the first time she could feel her difference.

She started to notice other things. Like when the Dairy Queen first opened and she and her friends went down to get ice cream. They got in line, and a few white people walked up behind them. The lady at the window asked Mary and the other Black kids to step aside for a minute so she could take the orders from the white customers first. "And we were children, so what are we supposed to say back to them?" Mary said. She knew that if she went home and told her mother what had happened, Pattie would have gone to the restaurant and told them off. Mary didn't say anything. She knew what had taken place was wrong. She also just wanted ice cream.

Despite the racism in Lowndes County, Mary felt seen, was seen. In her community, everyone looked out for everyone else, made sure the other was okay. There were always people who paid attention to her when the world around her took no meaningful stock. Here, she was not the Black girl; she was the sharp and rebellious girl who lived on Cemetery Road.

As a teenager in the late 1970s, Mary liked watching Westerns, admiring the scenery and interiors of the houses. She embroidered zodiac signs onto jeans and jackets to make a little money. And like her girlfriends, she read *Right On!* magazine obsessively to mimic the latest clothing and hair styles. When it was warm out, she and her friends hung out in the fields and picked plums. Their parents didn't let them stray far, so they congregated on the roads and in their private, wild domains of green. It was better than school. Mary did well in class, but she tried not to think about the future. Her two sisters were fourteen and fifteen years older, and they had left the house before she wanted them to go. She hated that they were gone. Mary felt abandoned: "I didn't really know what I wanted to do or wanted to be, because I didn't have anybody really to—I didn't have that guidance. Somebody to mold me and say you can be anything you want to be." Pattie pushed her, but being the ninth of ten children and the only girl at home forced Mary to make her own way. Her sisters had both gone with their young children to Detroit, where General Motors and other automobile companies had started hiring Black workers in the 1910s and '20s. They had realized that there was nothing in the Belt for them, and so they took off without so much as a look back. Her oldest brother also left to make his life in Detroit, working for General Motors. So many folks from the Belt moved to Michigan that the transplants joked that they had enough people to make up their own Alabama Town. Lowndes County expatriates started up Detroit branches of their home-town church and social clubs and created groups like the Detroit–Lowndes County Christian Movement for Human Rights, to send funds, food, clothes, and books to activists in Alabama.

Starting in 1900, nearly a quarter of Black Alabam-ians had begun to leave the Black Belt's chlorophyll-lit rural stretches and small towns for better opportunities in work, education, and housing. To find that elusive, slippery better life. For twenty years on, they went to Birmingham, which was firing on its steel industry, and to the Midwest and up north. Mary's parents decided to stay. They had some neighbors who left, catching trains and buses or, like one man they knew, taking their boss's truck to the store and never coming back. They were all headed to their next home. Some didn't make it, and everyone knew their stories: One man got on a train to escape being lynched, and his attackers stopped the train to pull him off and kill him. "A lot of people left running for their lives," Mary said. Her father's half sister had sent Mary's cousin, before Mary was even born, out of the Belt because a white man was supposed to be after her; she was a beautiful young woman. One of Bigg's sisters fought the policemen who came to repossess her furniture; she got ahold of their gun and chased them out, and then went to Brooklyn and never came back. Pattie's younger sister left home at the age of twenty-two, pregnant with the child of a married man. She followed him to Cleveland and died in childbirth. Pattie had to go to Cleveland to collect her baby niece, and she buried her sister not far from where the family house stood in Hayneville.

Mary believed the reason for most everything could be traced back to Scripture. "I ain't trying to sound like no religious fanatic, Lord, but I had to go back to the Scripture because I feel—" she trailed off. She leaned back in her chair and closed her eyes, telling herself, "Oh God, don't let me get emotional. Please, Jesus."

It was late 2021, and we were sitting in her comfortable, carpeted living room, with its dark and plush fabrics and cushions and family photos and mementos. Her mother, Pattie Mae, who was now hard of hearing but still sharp of mind, was in her motorized wheelchair nearby, both listening to us and watching the TV. They had celebrated her one hundredth birthday back in May. In the mornings, Mary said a little sheepishly, they had a routine after breakfast: they put on *Family Feud*, then the news, then *Family Feud* again. The news was on: a woman was shoving tater tots into her mouth for a competition. We watched for a moment in disgust.

When Mary opened her eyes after a long minute, they were wet and pink; she was crying anyway. "Some of the things I read in the Scripture, it matches up what I do; so I'm like, 'Okay, so I'm not wrong.' Even though sometimes it look like a person take your kindness for weakness, as long as you know you're doing it for the right reasons."

Her niece Ophelia couldn't understand sometimes why Mary extended herself so much, to so many people, to people who didn't really deserve it. "And let us not be weary in well doing: for in due season we shall reap, if we faint not," reads a Bible verse. Mary said, "It's not the reaping that I'm concerned about. The old folks used to say, 'It's in you. Why not do it?'" She didn't mean to get involved in public life and activism. "I first started working in the community back in ninety-nine, when our town needed a mayor," she said. In January of that year, the mayor at the time, a Black man named Joe Eddie Morgan, had resigned because of ill health. Two men began to share the position, one a white retired farmer named Ruben Haigler and the other a Black funeral home owner named Karl Bell, after the Hayneville town council appointed the farmer and the Democratic governor appointed Bell. The appointment of the farmer hit people the wrong way, after decades of illegitimate rule by white politicians of a mostly Black town, and Mary and other residents rallied for Bell's appointment. He was eventually designated the official mayor.

Mary, more than anything else, felt a sense of duty—to her mother and brother, who lived with her; to her community; to the land beneath her home—and this overpowered the other feelings, of anger, resentment, disappointment. But Mary came from a legacy of purpose.

It would be a waste to throw it aside. She wouldn't have known how. She wasn't an accidental anything.

There is a certain heroism in the stories of the people who left Alabama, whether as part of the Great Migration from 1916 to 1970, or before that, when things looked bad, and after that, when things didn't look much better. An academic on the same research fellowship I had at a think tank in New York once told me that his peers often said the people who hadn't left the South, who stayed behind, were foolish or idiotic. All the smart people had made a run for it. I had never heard that said before. What did that make of the people who arrived here after those who had left? And the people who returned after leaving? And the people who stayed put as they watched their kin and friends and lovers leave without them?

"We had fire in us," Mary said. "We've always had to fight, and I've watched my mother fight for everything." Not only for civil rights, but also to get Mary's brother Walter, who was disabled, into school, to ensure there was some dignity around them. You can't complain about what is going on around you if you aren't willing to do something about it. Through plantation slavery and Reconstruction, Jim Crow and the freedom movement, the Black Belt was used to dying and then being brought to life, as Veronica L. Womack writes in *Abandonment in Dixie*.

Mary would witness the next reincarnation.

CHAPTER FOUR

Between Blessing and Disaster

What Alabamians call the Black church down here began as a nesting doll of places. It was a scene of aspirations to a world better than this one. Beneath that, it was a site for fellowship and mutual practical support. On down, it was a location for organizing where members could plot in peace. The white church acted as a refuge for its members, too, but from evils that included the needs and desires of their Black fellow citizens: social integration, economic fairness, a seat at the table. White pastors and their congregations could avoid those demands while they worshipped.

I started going to church when I was a preteen, for a couple of years. Deeper Life Bible Church was technically a branch of a church that was well known in Nigeria—that was probably why my parents were drawn to it—and our pastor and his wife were Nigerian. But it was deeply southern in character. Most of the families who attended were Black, both African and American, and service fell along the lines of a Christian evangelical worship house. It was casual and familial and, back then, a center of my existence. For a kid growing up in Alabama, church was many a thing, but it was mainly a place to socialize and carry on the dramas begun earlier in the week at school. My friends talked about seeing one another at church events, hanging out at youth group, meeting boys at revivals and workshops. Not going to church was more harmful to our social health than our spiritual one.

The most desirable church out of the many in my hometown was called Frazer. Both Methodist and a megachurch before those became ubiquitous in the country, it had a television studio that broadcast its ministry years before my mom became hooked on the TV sermons of the pastor Joel Osteen. Frazer would also come to add gyms, recreation rooms, community halls, a bookstore, a coffee shop, and a water park on acres of green in East Montgomery. Its congregation was feathery white with specks of black and yellow. It was Christian mecca.

Church was one of the last frontiers of our segregated after-school life. During the day, we all gossiped in class, sat at the same lunch tables, and cut up on the playground. And when the last bell rang, we got onto buses or into our parents' cars—later our cars—and went different ways. We made plans for hangouts at the mall and in the parking lot of the Super Wal-Mart and at house parties where we knew we wouldn't see our friends of other races and didn't think much about it. That was how it was. When one of my white friends dated a mixed-race boy who went to a local private school, so many white kids at various schools talked shit about her that it would take my leaving Alabama for college in New Jersey before I saw that interracial dating shouldn't have been a taboo act. (Even then, I wasn't fully convinced; it still didn't happen all that often.) And in addition to the mall and the parking lot and someone's mom's house was the white church, from where stories would float the next week at school. Flirtations at youth group, hook-ups during lunch after service; I wanted to be a part of it. I daydreamed about what Frazer must be like: it was a place of faith, but also a house of adventure and sin. Black churches, including my own, just didn't have those qualities.

I finally got the chance to see Frazer when a high school classmate offered it up as a meeting place for our group project one evening; his family were members. But we went on a weeknight, and, as a result, it was anticlimactic. I took a bathroom break as a chance to wander the empty halls, looking into shadowy classrooms and out through polished windows. The place felt strangely bereft of life; even God seemed be at home, waiting until Sunday to get lit like everybody else. The boy who invited us was one of the most popular in my high school, where being performatively Christian and well liked went hand in hand. He was smart and sweetly funny and dated all the prettiest girls in high school, and he came out as gay years after he left Alabama for college.

When I went to Frazer another time, for a fund-raiser

for my speech and debate team one weekend, I found it similarly disappointing: wooden tables, brochures, dubious smiles, linoleum, fluorescence, concrete. Courtyards and flowers. None of the debauchery I had heard about. I recognized that what had attracted me to the church was darkly ironic: upstanding white members could use their affiliation as evidence of their goodness and righteousness. It was part of the idea that while they may not have agreed with certain beliefs and lifestyles, they didn't have hate in their hearts for anybody. But they also didn't generally want much to do with anybody else. Their shared pews and block associations and social circles were unapologetically homogenous. There was nothing to be sorry for if the alternative was inconceivable.

Adults of any race made sure to ask new acquaintances if they went to church, which one they went to, and if it was working out for them, before they got around to asking anything about them. So much of our religion was about testifying to our experiences of getting saved and loving Jesus and making sure that zeal caught on like wildfire, spreading through our blandly tidy subdivisions. Before class, we pledged allegiance to the flag and had a minute set aside so we could pray, learned about both the theories of evolution and intelligent design, and had to get permission slips signed by our parents to learn about our bodies and sex. (My parents refused to sign mine, no matter how much I begged, and when the week of lessons began, I was sent to a satellite trailer with one other kid as the lesson went on in our regular trailer. We sat there not looking at each other and cursing our fate of having to start middle school without knowing how to put on a condom.)

The question of abortion grazed beneath the surface of false-sounding talk about faithfulness and abstinence. We knew girls had sex and that their parents took care of it if things went wrong. I was the only one in my high school group of friends who was surprised that the boy I had a crush on was already sleeping with his girlfriend at her mom's house; she was thirteen.

Pastors liked to ask their parishioners if they had a personal relationship with God, and I did, insomuch as I thought about him when my family prayed together before we went to bed, and when I promised him my gratitude if he would do just one thing for me. I was excited whenever I learned a new way of approaching God: considering him as a loving though harsh uncle, as someone who created us but then got distracted on his phone, as a ruthless con of the imagination. It felt thrilling to be skeptical in a place where too many things were assumed about me by virtue of what I looked like, how I spoke, where I lived.

In Alabama, we exist at the border of blessing and disaster, and it is still easier to believe in divine protection than to worry about the things we can't control, like the tornadoes that strike our state more than almost anywhere else in the country. At school, we filed into the halls for scheduled drills, and then we balanced on our knees while holding our heads in our laps with our hands interlaced around our skulls until we got cramps. This was the exact position, our teachers said, that would keep us safe when tornadoes whipped through the building. What kind of logic they had used to determine this, I don't know, but we prayed for the best.

This is how the faithful here have always been. Better not to home in too closely on the details. As evangelicalism spread in the Deep South in the mid-eighteenth century, whether the denomination was Baptist, Presbyterian, Methodist, Episcopalian, or none at all, its shepherds were not concerned about which Christian sect their faithful claimed, as long as they professed allegiance to the white southern Christian tribe. Black people, Jews, Catholics, and other minorities could never be let in. The evangelical tenets were easily identifiable: fevered sermons, members being entwined in one another's lives, hard-and-fast (but readily excused if trespassed) rules for living, and ecstatic experience as king. As time passed, those who were excluded eventually made their way inside, taking practices that were private into the mainstream by guiding congregations with their own musical and preaching rituals, creating parallel spheres of worship and communion.

The Black church was also a means of defense. Black Alabamians had always determined their own spiritual fates. The church had been a site of resistance when they used it to gather and plan and sustain amid ever-closing-in walls of surveillance and criminalization. Plots after prayers. While enslaved, they worshipped in their quarters, apart from the white churches they were often forced to attend, and kept alive West African spiritual practices. Through Reconstruction and the civil rights movement, they used the worship house as a key place to strategize against campaigns of terror. And as time went on, for too many white Alabamians, church became an attempt to appropriate the moral high ground, not only to redeem themselves for past, shamefully public racial sins, but also to stake space on a new battlefield of family values. At least, this would prove to be winning political rhetoric.

The most hard-minded of the Christian faith, despite being in the minority of believers, had an outsize influence on poor states like Alabama by appealing to the basest emotions of its residents, Black and white and Native and immigrant. The feeling that God was on their side, but they could rarely catch up or get ahead. That God was working on their behalf, but the government certainly wasn't. And that the only way to make the government work for them was to force it to see the errors of its ways, to push it to a holier way of being. These beliefs resulted in a social conservatism that spanned racial identities. In 2014, 61 percent of white Alabamians supported making abortion illegal in most cases, as did 48 percent of Black Alabamians, the majority in both racial groups. Thirty-five percent of white Alabamians and 47 percent of Black ones said they were fine with legal abortion; the rest abstained. These close percentages, in a state where most Black people voted as Democrats and white people as Republicans, were not a coincidence; abortion was perhaps the foremost social issue on which evangelical Christians saw the need to exert their personal moral opinions. The most fundamentalist parishioners took this duty to the extreme, displaying the Ten Commandments in public spaces, lobbying for school prayer, and protesting for abstinence-only learning—some of the hallmarks of my public school education.

Two decades into the 1800s, Baptist churches in Alabama formed the Alabama Baptist Convention. As with most religious institutions in the country, its role was both spiritual and political. In 1823, four years after Alabama became a member of the union, but was still wild and in contest between its Native inhabitants and white settlers, the convention's first active members were missionaries. The Creek War had stripped Indians of much of their land, but the state still had the task of clearing way for its cotton enterprises and homesteads for the people who would run and work them. The Creek were in the way. Missionaries had a crucial part to play in the fray, and they set about teaching the Creek both Christianity and English in an effort to distance them from their culture and land. Sent by the enemy, the Red Stick warriors might have said.

The Creek had a history of turning away missionaries, like the Protestant ones from the Moravian Church, because many of them had no desire to convert to Christianity. But Creek leaders decided it would be useful to learn English and skills in tool manufacturing, gun making, and wood building, so they allowed some Christian craftsmen into their nation. The Creek also believed that the missionaries wanted them to be removed to Indian Territory. Over the eastern border in Georgia, state and federal officials had forced most of the Creek to leave the state by 1825; some of them came to Alabama, where, through the 1820s, both the Baptists and the Methodists had missions.

After Indian removal got going in Alabama, the Episcopalians set up a mission to attend to the remaining Poarch Creek. Stephanie Bryan went to an Episcopalian church as a girl and still claims the denomination to this day. "We had a very strong religious community," she told me with pride. "Very strong churches in this core community." Calvin Chappelle was confirmed in a Methodist church and now goes to an Episcopalian one. Mary McDonald grew up in, and still attends, Methodist churches, but as she said, "I always say it's nondenominational. It's just a Jesus church. It's just the pure word of God, right from the Bible." Still, Southern Baptists rule the state and are a defining part of its identity, even as 2021 marked the fourteenth year in a row that the membership of the Southern Baptist Convention fell. It had gone from about 16 million members in 2006 to 14 million. Being evangelical, which means they subscribe to the Gospels, or the story of Jesus, and believe in the importance of spreading that story to whomever they can however they can, is foundational to the religion and to the relationship between Alabamians and their faith. It is important to preach from suburban rooftops the ability of a person to give their soul to Jesus at any time, to be born again at sixteen or sixty-five. It is never too late.

According to the way Alabamians practice Christianity, usually with an evangelical flair, they have it right. Absolution is possible. So are forgiveness and reconciliation. Maybe not complete forgetting, but redemption is always around the bend. I don't remember exactly when I was saved at Deeper Life, but I do remember looking at the pulpit with satisfied superiority whenever the pastor asked for those parishioners who had not yet given their souls to God to come down and pledge them. He wasn't talking about me, even if I was always on the verge of going to hell.

Southern Baptists believe there will be a Judgment Day, a time when all of us will be evaluated by God to determine whether we will enter heaven or hell. When I first learned about the idea as a child, I panicked for years about how to balance my tally of daily sins with virtuous acts. I believed I was in constant danger of being sent on my way to hell if God suddenly showed up in Alabama. That fear seemed to me emblematic of how the people I grew up around thought of religion and why they needed it in their lives: fearing God's wrath was the best way to keep themselves, and others, in line. Not that the fear often worked. Fearing God, while welcoming his love, was supposed to remind us to be charitable, but the idea of charity seemed to extend only as far as the boundaries of conservative politics let it. We lived in a state that elected governors, after all, who refused to expand Medicaid to two hundred thousand people without health care, or to accept federal funding to provide food assistance for hungry schoolchildren during the summer. The Alabama Baptist Convention had the distinction of forming before the Southern Baptist Convention, which believers created in 1845 after splitting with Northern Baptists over their opposition to slavery. In May of that year, the Alabama Baptist Convention eagerly sent delegates to the first meeting of the regional group. The two associations grew in parallel, following the currents of slavery and Jim Crow. At the Southern Baptist Convention, slavery became an "institution of heaven," and

Black people descendants of Ham, Noah's wicked son from the Bible. Enslaved Alabamians were told they were divinely compelled to remain in their place below, ground down and run over. It was not surprising they got their own churches going as soon as they could; they managed to separate the feeling from the storytellers. It would take until 1995 for the Southern convention to apologize for defending slavery and perpetuating racism. Seventeen years later, the Southern convention elected its first Black president, a minister from New Orleans named Fred Luter. Luter liked to preach about the need for every believer to be a missionary to spread the Baptist word.

Luter, a descendant of enslaved people, led a church with more than seven thousand members before Hurricane Katrina drowned the building and many of his parishioners' homes, and he believed it was possible for Southern Baptists to be part of a national racial reconciliation, that healing was divinely compelled. He served two terms as president. But the fall after the George Floyd uprising, six years after Luter's presidency ended, the leaders of the convention's six seminaries issued a statement denouncing the legal concept of critical race theory, calling it "incompatible with the Baptist Faith and Message." Around the country, right-wing pundits and politicians were using the nonexistent threat of critical race theory being taught in schools to distract from the need for a racial reckoning, and the convention's statement appeared as a signal that it did not take the Black Lives Matter movement seriously. The statement very nearly sent much of its Black membership out the door, until an Alabama preacher showed up.

When Alabamian pastor Ed Litton was elected as the convention's president in 2021, it was a sign that, five years on, it was finally considering rejecting Trumpism. Litton's opponents included pastors who pushed for an extremism more aligned with the roots of Southern Baptists, and Litton narrowly won. For the past two presidential elections, most Southern Baptists had voted for Donald Trump, but Litton was different enough: while conservative, he believed the convention should be open about race and foster reconciliation. The group had been trying to attract Black Baptist churches in recent years, with little success, even though Black, Latino, and Native American congregations were growing the fastest within the denomination. Since Reconstruction, many Black Baptist congregations had been joining the National Baptist Convention, skipping the gatherings of their southern brethren. After the statement on critical race theory, Black churches countered the convention's invitation: Why join when the group pretended that racism was nonexistent or irrelevant? For decades, almost a third of the denomination's members had been enslaved people, and many of the other members had owned them; those beginnings had haunted the enterprise ever since. If the religion wanted to expand again, redeeming its past would have to be part of the work. Conditions are no longer to their advantage: to lure back Black, brown, and Native members, they need more than just the Bible and brute force. Frazer, the white Christian mecca in my hometown, now has a "Hispanic Ministry" with a Latino pastor and Spanish-language service.

To many Americans, Trump had seemed like an anomaly, a strange and scary sideshow that had come out of nowhere, with no warning before 2016, to lead us into decline. But to many down here, he was not all that unfamiliar. "The lone prominent American politician whose politics really matched Trump's was Jeff Sessions, the state's junior senator, and a strain of populist conservatism, often allied with an explicit sense of white victimization, stretches back throughout Alabama's political history," Benjamin Wallace-Wells writes in the *New Yorker*. "Religion, for politicians in this strain, and for Trump, often operated as another element of their identity politics." Trump's crudeness and blind stubbornness had long been a winning tactic to assume office in Alabama. His proclaimed religious beliefs—no matter that Trump's behavior was the opposite of pious—made those traits seem admirable. A brave soldier in God's army.

It was like when former Alabama governor Forrest Hood "Fob" James Jr., who served during the last half of the 1990s, despaired to the state board of education that creationism should be included in the school curriculum. To mock the idea that humans had come from apes, he pretended he was a monkey at the meeting. In 1996, biology textbooks in Alabama began carrying evolution disclaimers. They still do. James, who was named after his father and the Confederate generals Nathan Bedford Forrest and John Bell Hood, used state discretionary funds to send high school teachers the anti-evolutionary book *Darwin on Trial*. The education board meeting was during his second term as governor; during his first, in the '80s, he had won the office as a Democrat. He was the only governor in Alabama's history to be in office with two different parties. The first time, he called himself a "born-again Democrat." He was baptized again into the Republican Party in the early '90s, when he changed parties after previously losing two Democratic primaries.

Or it was like when Roy Moore was dismissed as chief justice of the Alabama Supreme Court because he refused to take down a statue of the Ten Commandments he had installed in the rotunda of the court building. His refusal became a righteous cause, the latest chapter in the Southern Crusades. Both Trump and Moore tested the loyalty of the most devout voters, who could no longer ignore that the two men had no mind for biblical values, no desire to personally uphold them. But the saving grace of these politicians, and the ones that came before them, was that they opposed abortion and talked about the taking of innocent lives with a fervor that seemed real, or real enough.

It is normal in Alabama for someone you just met to launch into a friendly soliloquy on God's love as introductory conversation and then, once they ask for and get your phone number, not to leave you alone for weeks afterward until you come to visit their church at least once—and then, after you visit, not to leave you alone until you confirm that you are joining their church or have settled on another one. And then, if you have joined another church, to tell you to make sure and let them know if it doesn't work out for you. Recently, I was at an airport in New York, on my way to Charlottesville, decades after I had regularly attended a church. I was sitting next to a woman who casually asked her neighbor, a woman with whom she had only exchanged pleasantries about our delayed flight, and whose name I was sure she did not know, "How could you not want God's love? It's just so good!" I kept turning to look at her speak. It felt like home.

My parents decided to leave our church after we had been attending long enough to know most of the other members, and for them to know us. From then on, when people asked what church we went to—a question deemed as essential to knowing the character of a person as the kind of family they came from—my parents would tell them we were still looking for a new one. We tried one or two others on the occasional Sunday, but it never felt right, at least to me, to be in a church in the same way again. But it was impossible to say that we were done with church altogether. When I asked my dad years later, he explained that he and my mom had gotten sick of our pastor's hypocrisy, especially when he started preaching to his Black, working- and middle-class congregation that they should vote for local evangelical Republican candidates whose platforms did nothing for Black Alabamians. That hypocrisy, whether about sex or politics, is what can be disturbing about going to church down South. Both my parents had gone to Catholic school as kids, saved before they could talk, but they found intolerable the zealous piety at too many churches that tried their best to ignore the cruelties of race and class.

Mary, in the Black Belt, knows that piety well. The pastor at her current church is white. "Most of the congregation is white," she told me. "And they *white*. You know what I'm saying?" I laughed. "They still white, you get me?" Mary went on, "God will use who he choose to bring forth his Word. So, a lot of people wonder why I go to hear the Word from a white man. Because it's God's Word, and God put me there to hear it." She is no fool about who is telling the story, but she knows how to separate the feeling from it.

CHAPTER FIVE

Forced Closeness

The hierarchy of the Old South kept out both Black and poor white people by design, and the fictions of color kept the latter from uniting with the former. Many Alabamians had indeed not owned slaves, but the privileges of whiteness made class inequities easier to bear. They may have had no money, but at least they weren't niggers. When slavery eased into sharecropping and tenant farming, Black and poor white Alabamians bore the burden of making the lives of their landed white neighbors close to what they were before the war. And so the three groups often lived and worked more closely together in the Deep South than in most other places in this country. Their shared landscape was disfigured by bigotry, but also shaded with intimacy and an assumption of mutual understanding. We like to think we still keep everyone close here, enemies and otherwise, and that gives us comfort.

The intimacy manifested in different forms. There was the forced closeness of slavery, when Black Alabamians had to keep every part of themselves open to their white masters. When white Alabamians, slave-owning or not, could extract whatever comforts they wanted from whichever Black people were around. In the late summer days of 2017, I went to a rally for a new Confederate memorial dedicated to "Unknown Alabama Confederate Soldiers," held in a private park outside my hometown. I had just started reporting in Alabama again and had spent so much time out of the state that I grew nervous on the morning drive to the park. I wondered if people would be hostile to me, if I would be the only Black person there, if I was putting myself in danger. I had reported in African war zones, but felt more uneasy on that country road. News reports in New York were talking about white extremism in the South all the time. As I got close to the park, I couldn't find the place. I made a loop around and saw a television news truck parked on the side of the road. I stopped to talk to the crew, which included a Black female reporter, and they told me the rally organizers wouldn't let them in. I commiserated with them and then asked for directions. It turned out we were right in front of it. As I pulled up to the entrance, I saw a group of men in camouflage with guns patrolling the area. The man at the gate looked inside the car at me, asked me if I had any cameras. When I said I didn't, he waved me inside. Joining the other attendees standing in a loose crowd in front of the small stage, I seemed to be the only Black person there, and everyone seemed to know it. After the speeches were over, people came to me.

A wiry white woman with blond hair got to me first. She told me how glad she was that I had come, which I actually appreciated, until she kept talking. I had to see, the woman went on, how the people in attendance were not about hate. She told me that her own ancestor had been so close with her slaves she taught them to read from the Bible. Lessons out in the fields. The woman said she took this as a sign of love. Later on, I saw a mixed-race girl wearing an antebellum hoop-skirted dress, chaperoned by women who belonged to a group called the Order of Confederate Rose. The girl's white mother, in a too-tight similar dress, told me, a little defensively, that enslaved people had fought for the Confederacy, too. She rambled on for a while about how it had been tough for her family to accept her Black former partner, but that they loved her daughter. A man with a brown ponytail came up to us and began his own monologue. He told me that the brutality of slavery hadn't stopped his people from thinking of their slaves as kin. One of his ancestors put down the names of enslaved children in his family ledger. The man said this with pride as he searched my eyes for understanding. I couldn't give it to him, and he could tell. When he tried to explain more, I politely said I had to get to other people. Everyone I spoke with seemed desperate for confirmation that the forced closeness of their ancestors' interracial relationships had meant some-thing—if not redemption, then at least salvation. When once asked to name the greatest period in American history, Roy Moore responded that it would have to be the pre–Civil War era because "it was great at the time when families were united—even though we had slavery—they cared for one another."

There was the reluctant nearness of labor that followed emancipation, the consuming domestic service of Black women in white homes and the bitter land tenure of Black sharecroppers and tenant farmers that made the exploitation of slavery appear only slightly more ruinous. The fountain of white paternal benevolence (not run dry after thanksgiving with the Creek) continued to drip through the currents of communities where poor and working-class Black and white folks lived together. Things were fine as long as Black people knew their place. When they didn't, or they listened to outside agitators, was when problems arose.

Before I left the rally that afternoon, another attendee, who admitted she was originally from north of the Mason-Dixon line, made sure to tell me that the NAACP—founded by a "white socialist," she said—had caused the worst of "our" racial troubles down here.

The rally took place in Crenshaw County. Two hundred miles north of Crenshaw is Gadsden, a hilly city in the green fur–covered mountains of Upper Alabama. Tina Johnson's mother, Katherine, grew up near there without much, and she told Tina and her other children to stay away from Black kids: not to be ugly to them, but to stay away. That was how it was in the 1960s and '70s. The family lived outside Gadsden, way out in the country, in a place where they could roast marshmallows in their yard if they wanted to and not worry about neighborhood association rules. They did all their own work, home improvement, repairs. Katherine couldn't read or write, but she knew how to make money. She could leave the house with ten dollars and come back with a hundred because she had bought a gallon of paint and painted someone's house. She was an electrician—it was a mystery as to how she'd gotten her license—and drove diesel trucks and farmed. She was also clawing through the wilds of undiagnosed mental illness, Tina believed, with frequent manic episodes.

Tina was scrappy. She was a beautiful girl, with blond hair and radiant blue-green eyes that didn't seem God-given. But they were, and so was her politeness, and openness, and tolerance for all the worst-behaving men in the world, fathers and lovers alike.

Various men moved in and out of their home, but the one who kept coming back was named Griffin, and he was the man Tina considered her dad. He was reserved, never smoked or drank, and had a hard time showing his love. There was a limit to how close he let people get, but Tina could feel that he cared for her. He was an electrician and an entrepreneur. And a little off: "A lot of people call crazy people that's got money eccentric, but if you ain't got no money, you're crazy. Daddy had a touch of crazy," Tina said. His family had lost nearly everything during the Great Depression, and Griffin took to hiding money in spare tires, milk jugs, couch cushions—Tina once found a stack of hundred-dollar bills and was giving them away at school before a teacher stopped her. Katherine yelled at her for being so reckless, but she would keep Griffin's money whenever she found it herself. Griffin spoiled Tina, gave her money when she wanted it. But it was her mother who taught her how to get it from him. It was much later that Tina realized, "It ain't worth the trouble. With Daddy, you had to practically con him. I didn't like playing those games. But Mama knew how to use those men. She was good at brainwashing them." It felt to Tina like an exhausting ritual of flattery and passive-aggressiveness. But that was how she learned to be a woman: *Never give it up*—she was a pretty girl and had a gold mine between her legs, everyone told her—*and know how to get what you want from a man*. When her mother felt like a man was no longer serving her, bowing to her and her children's needs, she was through with him. Katherine was mean, but she was ambitious and knew how to get ahead. She was the smartest woman Tina has ever known. Tina watched her.

Katherine was born in Detroit at the tail end of the Depression. Her father worked for Ford, and he went back and forth between the bleached-white sandstone of Sand Mountain, the tornado-prone nook of Alabama where the family lived, and Detroit. The family thought of themselves as poor, but they were also the first ones in their neighborhood to have electric lights. You could say Sand Mountain was where Katherine spent her childhood, but that was a sliver of the truth. She got married at twelve years old to a disc jockey at a radio station, the first of six times she would end up marrying. Tina's grandfather was a hard man. He beat his kids, and his children seemed to have done whatever they could to get free from him. His sons went into the army, some enlisting as young as fourteen. They were all just babies.

Katherine and the disc jockey had three kids, Tina's

oldest half brothers and sisters. They divorced when Katherine was in her early twenties because he cheated on her and left her for another woman. Katherine was not a single mother for long before she married another man, with whom she had Tina's older brother. She would later give Tina that husband's surname, but they were not related. Katherine had Tina while having an affair with a married man who worked for the local John Deere tractor company. Tina remembered that he was a drunk and seemed to have a lot of money that Katherine gladly took. He paid for Katherine's prenatal care, and when Tina first came home from the hospital, she was dressed in brand-new clothes and blankets. That was the one time he did right by Tina. She didn't know he existed until she was twelve, when Katherine took her to see him. It was devastating. Tina would come to feel that her mother took it out on her that he hadn't left his wife and married Katherine.

Maybe he could have looked out for Tina. Her uncle, who was married to Katherine's sister, began abusing her when she was five and didn't stop touching her until she was twelve. Around the same time, Katherine's brother was hurting her, too. It started with him taking Tina to his darkroom, putting her on his lap, and rubbing between her legs. Tina thought that must be the way the photos were developed. It made her feel like dirt. She ran from him whenever she saw him. Fortunately, she didn't see him much. Tina knew he was hurting her cousins in the room next to the one he shared with his wife. The one night she slept over, her ten-year-old cousin insisted that she lie on the inside of the bed the two girls were sharing. When her uncle came into the room later that night, Tina realized why. She turned over and faced the wall, another cousin lying still in the bunk bed above them, until he left. The bedroom had no door and Tina was sure her aunt knew.

But when it came to sexual abuse, you didn't talk about it. "It's drilled in from birth, you don't talk about sex at all," Tina said. You were supposed to submit to what a man wanted, especially if he had some means about him. There was no such thing as being violated by a powerful man. Girls like Tina were not expected to be helpless anymore—that was a thing of the past—and her mother taught her how to shoot. Katherine owned a rifle, with which she could practically shoot a silver dollar two miles off, and she tried to show her kids how to use a shotgun. (Tina couldn't stand all the guns her mother owned, though; she was afraid of them.) But doing what was proper was taken seriously. Tina could get an education, which she did, and get a job, which she did, but pleasing the men in her life was the final say on her value.

The abuse from Katherine's brother-in-law stopped only because Tina got mad. She was washing dishes in the kitchen one day, after a family gathering at her house. All the other kids and the adults were outside talking and getting ready to leave. Their dog was lapping at Katherine's feet. Tina's uncle came back inside and put his hands on her vagina as she did the dishes. She happened to be cleaning the iron skillet, and before she knew what she was doing she hit him in the head with it. As she turned to face her bleeding uncle, she grew terrified: she thought her mother was going to beat her to death.

"I was more scared about getting a whooping than realizing what I had done," Tina recalled. Her uncle went outside bleeding and Tina's aunt was trying to stop the blood and all Tina could think was that she was going to get killed. That's what her uncle had always said: if she told anybody what he was doing to her, she would get beaten, her mom would get hurt. Tina went outside with her head down, nearly shaking. It was the first time she truly understood that what her uncle had been doing to her was wrong. But she didn't know if anybody else would see it like that. Her uncle told the group that he had hit his head, and Tina could relax a little. He never touched her again.

The first time Tina and I met, I pulled up to the house she shared with her husband in a pleasant mountainside neighborhood in Gadsden. I had gotten her contact information from another journalist, and then Tina and I had briefly spoken on the phone and texted. But when she opened the door, I could have sworn she was taken aback. She seemed stiff, a little nervous. As I followed her into the living room and then the kitchen for a glass of water, I wondered if she was surprised that I was Black; all she knew about me by at that point was that I worked at the *New Yorker*. She gave me water in a big plastic cup. We sat down on her couch, and I opened my notebook, thinking through how I could get her to relax. I asked her about her most recent husband, a man named Morris whom she had married in 2010 after knowing him for two weeks, and about her beloved stepdaughters, one of whom lived nearby with her own kids. She got up to show me photos, smiling big. I looked politely. Tina's husband was Black; so were her stepchildren. She was ill at ease, I realized, because I was a stranger in her house. Her husband is stingy, she later told me, and makes her reuse their red plastic cups and Styrofoam plates. Now in her fifties, she is still beautiful, frosted blond hair and those startling, unreal eyes. The soft lilt to her voice is so soothing that you can almost miss the hard edges around what she is saying.

As a girl, Tina soon told me, she was at her best when she was outside, helping her mother with the farming and taking care of their goats, pigs, and cows. "I don't want to say it like this, baby, but I'm gonna say it: we were like the Black folks," Tina said. "We didn't have the opportunities that white folks had." Every year, they grew a crop on land her mother leased. One year, they had green peppers, another sugarcane. They didn't have any equipment, so they cut down the sugarcane and stripped it themselves, took it to the mill so it could be turned into syrup, and then used the money to go on vacations to Disney World and Yellowstone. They took care of themselves; that was the important thing. Tina's mother was nothing if not resourceful. She would go to the potato house and collect a truckload of the inferior ones that had been cut or nicked and wouldn't sell. She stored them in the basement with limes on them, and the family ate potatoes for months.

It was decades later that Tina would meet a son of her father's, a product of his marriage, and learn more about the people in the backward-reaching corridor from which she came. Her great-great-grandfather was known for being part of the effort to remove Cherokee Indians from northern Alabama. He was a ranking officer in the military and helped move them to Indian Territory whether they wanted to go or not. "They pushed them all out," Tina said. Despite that, her great-great-grandfather was said to have taken a Cherokee wife and settled in Arizona. He never came back. Tina's father's family was said to have a lot of Indian blood. On her mother's side, the story was that her grandmother's people were heavily Indian, too. Dutch immigrants made up the people her grandfather could directly call ancestors. It could seem like a tangle of origin stories, but there was a pattern to the family tales Tina's elders had passed on. Because some of her ancestors had made their lives with Indians, they would forever be the kind of white people who could not get ahead.

Tina and her siblings didn't do sports and activities like some of the other kids, so they made their own fun. They ran around, went to the lake and made mud pies, climbed fruit trees to eat or sell the fruit, and busted open watermelons on their neighbors' field to eat the hearts. ("We were taught that if you ate it in the field, it wasn't stealing," Tina said. To this day, it is hard for her to eat watermelon because she ate so much of it back then.) They always found something to do. Her stepfather bought her a Volkswagen Bug when she was twelve, and Tina drove all over the mountain in it. But at school, she gave everybody hell. She was full of rage. Rage about the abuse and about how powerless she felt. She was smart but had no interest in class, had no time for it.

Tina got her first boyfriend at thirteen; James was around seventeen. Her mother hated him. Tina was afraid of sex and in no rush to do it. But she was in love with James, and so decided to sleep with him when she was sixteen. She got pregnant that first time. As soon as she found out she was pregnant, the couple agreed that they had to get married, even though Katherine had already told Tina that she would never give her permission to do so. Tina and Katherine were brawling all the time over James and Tina sneaking out of the house to see him. It took her a long time to get out from under the hand of her mother. Katherine had controlled all her children with frightening intensity. The men, the control—that was survival to Katherine. She was a self-made woman, but it often seemed like the men in her life got more out of the relationships than she did. They got affection and sex and freedom to leave whenever they wanted.

Tina learned fast what types of men were perverts. "It'll make you cry. 'Cause when you see that look on them, you know it. You know it. And it's something you never forget," she said. It was a man wanting to take what was hers without asking. Like that Christian bastard Roy Moore.

Roy Moore was dismissed as chief justice of the Alabama Supreme Court by the state's Court of the Judiciary in 2003 because he refused to take down his five-thousand-pound Ten Commandments monument in the judicial building. But fifteen years later, Alabama voters approved a constitutional amendment that gives officials and institutions the right to display the Ten Commandments in public settings. The constitution of the

state of Alabama may be the most wide-ranging in existence, with amendments covering matters from whether
public officials should be able to display the Ten Commandments to how to expand the right to bear arms, and
regulations concerning mosquitoes, litter, duels, prostitu-
tion, the catfish industry, and bingo games. It is certainly
among the most racist. An attorney named John B. Knox,
from the city of Anniston, smack-dab in the middle of the
route from Birmingham to Atlanta, was the president of
the 1901 constitutional convention. On the second day,
he announced calmly, and to no complaints, the need for
the men gathered to "establish white supremacy in this
state." It was one of the least controversial goals of the
convention. They produced a web of rules to ensure that
Black Alabamians could not exercise their rights as citizens, much less their right to vote.

Voters had to pass a literacy exam, unless they or their
ancestors had served in the military; white folks who
could not read or write could often avoid the test, but
Black people, whose enslaved forefathers had been
banned from serving, had to take it however white reg-
istrars presented it to them. Voters also had to pay a poll
tax, a fee to vote, before registering. Afraid of Black support of Republican Party liberals, and of growing white
support in northern Alabama for populist politicians who
rallied the working class, the convention aimed to prevent those groups from ever casting a ballot again. Their
rules disenfranchised Black and poor white people. In
fact, more white Alabamians ended up being excluded
from the vote than Black ones. Collateral damage for the
cause. (A federal court repealed the state poll tax in 1966.)

There were 155 delegates at the constitutional convention. All 155 were white men. Most worked in law and
banking. A quarter of them had served in the Civil War.
This was not unusual in the country at the time, but the
end result of the convention escaped sense. The constitution shut out Black Alabamians from the democratic process, yet a majority of them had somehow cast a vote in
favor of the document. According to white officials in the
Black Belt, Black voters there had ratified the constitution.
That kind of voting math would become a regular feature
of life in the state for decades to come.

About those populists: As the federal government
undertook austerity measures after the Civil War, depressed
prices for cotton created acute suffering for farmers of all
races, but the downturn radicalized a certain segment of
white ones. Prices for other crops were falling, and ship-
ping rates on the railroad were rising without limit. After
Reconstruction came to a close, and wealthy planters and
businessmen retook control of the state government, the
populists' formation of the Alabama's People's Party in
the 1890s drew in small farmers, sharecroppers, and industrial workers like Birmingham's coal miners. For the first
time, labor and class were the organizing principles of a
political movement here, instead of race. Northern Alabama held the heart of populist support in the state, for
good reason. The area had fiercely resisted Alabama's
seceding and going to war; of the some 2,600 Alabamians who served in the Union Army—you heard right—
most of them were from northern Alabama. They made
up a small percentage of the population and were mostly
farmers who did not own enslaved people. They opposed

the war for a variety of reasons: they felt it would spell carnage and disaster; they felt seceding was treason and would dishonor the American Revolution and their ancestors; and they felt the practice of slavery was not enough to risk economic ruin.

The Union would use its favor in the north to attack Alabama through the Tennessee River and the railroad lines that wound down south. After Alabama voted to secede, local Unionists and their families were ridiculed, scorned, at times punished and harmed, and were out of place in a state that was beginning to realize its odds of winning and needed somebody to blame. Some dissenters were called before community vigilante groups for questioning and threats, others found themselves on the margins of a home that was no longer welcoming. But as the war dragged on, deserters from the Confederate Army who were tired from battle, from seeing their relatives barely survive back home, and from recognizing that the men dying around them didn't include the wealthy planters who had led the secession charge, were also crossing over to the Union side. Either that or ducking out of service altogether. When the war ended, many of the Unionists joined the Republican Party. And during Reconstruction, they used the promise of an integrated state government to move into political life.

Unsurprisingly, not an exceeding amount about the Alabama Unionists exists in the public record; known as scalawags—that term was most of what I was taught— when they joined the Reconstruction-era state government, and being neither Confederates nor abolitionists, they're a footnote to the story. In my U.S. history class in high school, I didn't have time to wonder about these vaguely traitorous men who, for some reason, had cast their lots with the enemy, before we moved on to the next lesson. But it wasn't such a leap from opposing secession to then supporting, if with mixed feelings, the multiracial politics of Reconstruction, to reading the *People's Protest*, a newspaper in Cullman County. In 1893, the paper wrote, "We believe that every citizen, whether rich or poor, is entitled to the rewards of his labor." The People's Party supported civil liberties for Black Alabamians. Its three-time candidate for governor between 1890 and 1894, Reuben Kolb, a man with a handlebar mustache, said he would protect their legal and political rights, despite having commanded a Confederate artillery unit. The party faced blatant attempts at fraud by the Democrats. Even so, during the 1890s, it won two congressional elections in Alabama, in districts spanning northern Hill Country and the Black Belt. But its goals of increasing funding for public schools, ending the private leasing of convicts, and offering assistance to poor farmers would not be enough to overcome the Democrats' voter intimidation and manipulations of the two-party system. By 1900, its candidates no longer won races, and the party fell apart. Some populists in the north formed a progressive wing of the Republican Party, and others in Birmingham became Socialists. From then on, farmers and workers had to organize independently to protect their interests, like the radical Alabama Sharecroppers Union, a communist trade union led by Black sharecroppers in the 1930s.

The constitution of the state of Alabama may be the

most strikingly unjust when it comes to taxation and representation. It certainly is the most transparent about its injustice. As Wayne Flynt, a retired history professor at Auburn University, once told a journalist, "The motive for the 1901 constitution is fairly simple. People who had lots of property didn't want to pay property taxes." He went on: "And the best way to make sure they didn't pay property taxes was to make sure that no African-American voted, because African-Americans didn't own a lot of property and, therefore, were anxious to tax it in order to provide decent public schools—not only for their own children, but for white children as well." The tax code is regressive and defiant of the common good: the attempt to let rich Alabamians evade paying taxes on their property seeped into ways of letting them avoid paying taxes on their salaries and business income. Instead, their poor neighbors have to pay them. The bottom 40 percent of Alabamians pay 10 percent of their incomes in taxes; the top 1 percent pay less than 4 percent. The poorest here also spend almost eight times as much a share of their income than the best-off on the sales tax, which is among the highest in the country and is even put on groceries. This is by design. Local governments make almost half their revenue from sales and receipts taxes.

But the power of county governments to decide their own affairs—school boards on public education, health boards on hospitals and clinics, gas and water authorities on communal utilities, and economic development agencies on industry and investment—is in the hands of the state legislature. Counties have to go to the legislature to get approval to take local actions, either through

constitutional amendments that the whole state has to
vote to approve, or through legislative acts. To say it
in other words, most of the reason the constitution has
been amended so many times is to let county governments do the business of governing; nearly one-third of
those amendments concerns just one county, like letting
Etowah County hold flea markets on Sunday, or allowing
Limestone County to dispose of dead farm animals and
Fayette County to repeal its bounty on beaver tails. The
origins of this chaotic order lie in the period right after
white liberals and Black people held office in the state
during Reconstruction, when the antebellum ruling class
retook power in the capital and tried to make sure any
lingering dissenters in county seats had no real control.

In 2001, Flynt, the historian, was part of a push to hold
a public referendum on the constitution. Those opposed to
the referendum claimed it was a plot to remove the phrase
"under God" from the document, but Flynt and others
sued state officials on the grounds that the constitution
was illegitimate because, back in 1901, voter fraud had
allowed its ratification. They wanted a fair public vote or
a new document altogether. They were right, but they lost.

My proposed amendment: Alabama has had other
constitutions, including one ratified during Reconstruction in 1868. Eighteen of the one hundred convention
delegates were Black. The document is one of the most
enlightened the state has ever seen: it protected the rights
of all citizens, like that of Black people to vote; guaran-
teed funding for public education; and preserved the
property rights of married women. It was in place for

seven years, until Reconstruction ended and the Democrats threw it out.

My second proposed amendment: Booker T. Washington, president and cofounder of the Tuskegee Normal and
Industrial Institute, located east of Montgomery, wrote a
letter to Knox, the convention president, "representing
the feelings and wishes of the colored people of the State
of Alabama." Washington wrote that the letter was sent
out of an "earnest desire to be of some assistance in the
performance of a grave and perplexing task"—the duty
of drawing up the framework that would govern both
white and Black citizens, the latter of whom, as Washington pointed out, had cleared the woods, built the
highways and railroads, cultivated the lands, worked the
mines and farms, performed the domestic service, and
enlisted in the Confederate Army for white men like
them, men who were now debating their humanity. He
further wrote, "Almost for the first time since freedom
came to us, a law-making body assembles in the South,
bearing the supreme law-making power of the state, and
is left free to act entirely untrammeled by outside influ-
ences. Almost for the first time, the Negro is to rest his
future in a large degree upon the conscience and intel-
ligence of a great law-making body of a great Southern
state. You have the power. The world will watch while
you act.

"We are all owners of property and tax payers," he
went on. "And have the same interest in good government that you have."

It turns out there was a Black voice at the convention,

after all. It was exceedingly rational and forgiving. It was ignored, pushed to the postscript, but it is there.

* * *

In the nineties and early aughts, neighborhoods and schools were the most transparent indicators of how well the family of a child did and what that child could, as a result, do in Montgomery. How well they could move within its most valued institutions and how much they could expect to get from those places: academic prizes, athletic titles, social prestige. Among kids in the well-placed spheres, the girls and boys tended to speak the same, in entitled and unhurried drawls that sped up for no one. They dressed nearly the same: preppy, in pale cottons and linens. And they engaged in the same social activities, gathering to drink and party in the privacy of their family homes when their guardians were out of the house or choosing not to look. Their hangout spots in town were unglamorous but popular—the mall; the movie theater, which was in the mall; and then the food court, also in the mall. Activities where Black and white kids came together, like sports teams, band, and Girl Scouts, had unspoken rules that we learned as we went along. I belonged to a Girl Scout troop led by the mother of my friend Rachel; she and most of the troop were white. The racial makeup of our troop was not something I ever thought much about, because I considered Rachel a close friend, and her mother was affectionate to me.

But I soon learned the most important rules, that there was an invisible boundary determining how far I socialized with my white friends. We never went to the same parties, slept over at the same houses. The only times we shared rooms were at hotels during speech and debate team trips, in my experience, or in cabins on Scout camping weekends. The distrust went both ways: when a friend asked me to sleep over at her house in junior high, my parents refused to let me go, both because they said my friend had an older brother and because the family was white and unknown to them, though they never said the second thing. But a Girl Scouts sleepover they allowed. They had met Rachel's mom after past meetings and were comforted by the idea of a group of girls tucked away in sleeping bags in Rachel's living room. The morning after the sleepover—a night in which I took off all my clothes in my sleeping bag to make the girls laugh and then quickly pulled them all back on when Rachel's mom returned to the room—Rachel's mother separated us into groups of two or three to take showers together. She put the other Black girl, whom I barely knew, and me into the same bath. As Rachel's mom turned on the shower and sat by the tub, the other girl and I squirmed quietly under the water as we scrubbed ourselves with soap and glanced at each other with shyness and curiosity. When my mom arrived to pick me up and I got into the car, I told her about the segregated bath. She asked if anything bad had happened while we bathed, then nodded after I said nothing had. She had been in Alabama long enough to know most of the rules already.

The white members of socially elite circles had coming-of-age rituals, and their Black counterparts had almost the same ones: parallel cotillions and emerging-into-society ceremonies. A Black social club called Jack and Jill of America, founded by a group of twenty Black mothers during the Great Depression, gave well-off Black children their own chance to participate in cultural and community activities together and to network. Tastes and snobberies were passed down with equal opportunity on both sides of the color line. On the Black side, so were preferences for lighter skin, straighter hair, and a respectability that cared about white acceptance but pretended not to.

I was the child of immigrants who cared nothing about my entering any kind of society. On the sidelines of the two worlds, I watched them with fascination and envy for the ease their inhabitants had in their identities. From where I stood, white and Black privilege looked like kissing cousins.

CHAPTER SIX

Between Hunger and Desire

Alabamians crave meaning, through God, through sports, through family. Nobody judges you for it. There are times in a person's life that can take her years to determine their meaning. For Mary McDonald, it was falling in love. "I heard T. D. Jakes say one time, 'You ought to look back and just thank God for slamming some of those doors in your life,'" she said. "And that's one door I thank God for slamming in my life."

Mary was still a kid when she met Mark her senior year of high school; he had recently moved down from Cincinnati. They both came from big families: the thirteen kids in his house nearly matched the ten in hers. "Everything changed," she recalled. "I had it backward; I thought I should be able to pick who I want." Her family was old-fashioned: she wasn't allowed to go around with boys, much less date them. When Pattie forbade her from even going to ball games, Mary became a cheerleader so she could be there. But what she saw of the relationships around her—her parents, aunts and uncles, neighbors— she didn't like. To her eyes, the unions looked like a "sophisticated form of slavery." The women did everything for their men. Pattie, who had no competition for being the most devoted mother in the world, could barely take it. She woke up every Sunday morning to a house full of kids and then had to do all the cooking and the cleaning. Bigg sat back, meanwhile, with his legs crossed and an eye toward the television. In due time, he would tell his wife he needed his clothes, like he couldn't get them himself. That way of thinking repelled Mary. She went looking for something different and found her first boyfriend.

"I was young and in love—seventeen and in love," she said. The couple barely had time to themselves except at school; they couldn't go to the movies alone or anything. Mark's parents were also strict. They did let him come down to Mary's porch so the two could sit and talk and look at each other and let their hands touch; slow, hot moments still burned into her memory. Bigg disliked Mark, or the idea of him, so the couple would peel off and walk down the road a little. Decades later, Mary thought she probably would have ended up in a bad place had their relationship lasted. She couldn't exactly say how, but it had to do with her wanting a kind of love that was unlike what she saw around her and thinking she had it—but then realizing she had been fooled. For a while, there was the promise of something more freeing than what her parents had, love as a means to liberate herself. It made her nearly lose her head. Ulti-mately, all she knew for sure was that Mark ended up serving time in prison and then died there at the age of thirty-four. Some neighbors said he had passed because he was sick, but Mary believed he had been beaten to death. She didn't know why he had been sent there, but she still remembered the year he died, 1996, because it was the year he was supposed to turn thirty-five, another date she recalled like it was her own birthday. When Mark died, thirteen years had gone by since they broke up. "I had put a lot of distance between us," she said. "I'm the type of person, when I'm done with something, I am done. I can't go back, I won't let myself go back."

But Mary could frame the story of her life around that relationship. She and Mark graduated high school at the start of June 1979. Practically right after the ceremony, Mark went into the service. Mary enrolled in business college in Montgomery and settled in to wait for his return, until that Christmas. Her older brother came home from Michigan for the holidays every December, and after the one of 1979, she impulsively got into his car with some of her things and went back there with him. She had to quit college and explain to her bewildered parents why she needed to go, but the move made sense in her head. All her older siblings had gone to Michigan to make their own ways, and home had begun to feel suffocating. "I just wanted to breathe," she remembered. She would live in Pontiac, about thirty miles north of Detroit, and get a job in insurance in the city of Rochester; that was the easy part. She wanted a new experience and—it sounded like a line out of a novel but was true, she said—to "see the world." Traveling was educational. It was strategic, too. While she was waiting for Mark to return from the service, she could see what it was like to leave Alabama and do what all those people she had heard stories about had done since before she was born: get out of the Black Belt, see if there was something better out there than what they already knew.

But unlike her siblings and family friends, Mary would not get stuck up north. The plan was always to come back. The newness and the chill of that year still felt thrilling to remember. Mary liked her work. She lived right across from the Silverdome stadium and went to Detroit Lions games in the white cold and spent time with her siblings and nieces and nephews. She was a country girl on an adventure, used to waking up at six in the morning and stepping outside to breathe in the fresh air. There was little of that in Michigan, but she could look around and feel like she was trying on a life that could be hers if she wanted.

She did return to Hayneville, though, the seat of Lowndes County, where she had grown up in that roomy house next to the weeping willow. "It was just too cold; it wasn't for me," she said. "I liked being out on acres. I'm just not a city-life girl. Not only just there: I don't think I can live in the city anywhere. And I was in love with this guy." When she got back to Alabama from Michigan, and Mark then got back from the service, he told her he had met someone else. He was leaving her for another girl. Mary was not entirely surprised, it had always seemed too pure to be real, but it was no less devastating. She had no choice but to keep living with her parents and look for work. She got a job on a production line making military uniforms for $9.45 an hour, well above minimum wage at least. She worked efficiently: she was burning that sewing machine up, Mary said. Not long after, she started working for the state as a clinic coordinator, running family planning and childcare programs, doing the work of more than one person and doing it well. She never went back to college, never really thought about enrolling again after losing Mark. Later on, she would begin to wish someone had insisted she go back, stop running to the gym after work and, instead, run to school. Because she was smart: she was drawn to numbers, was skilled with them, and her memory was astounding. Mary could recall the most mundane things, like bank account numbers. Once, she rattled off Bigg's Social Security number to me, years after he had died. She then looked at my tape recorder and said with a mock gasp and a smile, "Oh Lord, I'm recording." But back then, she could reason that she was saving money and helping her parents, and that was worth something.

Mary is warm. She sees everything, but generously doesn't let on that she does, and her house is homey, if melancholic. Her elderly mother and disabled brother, Walter, drifted around the living room in their motorized wheelchairs, occasionally making sounds and comments that Mary good-naturedly responded to. She was their primary caretaker, but I never heard her complain, even when she wasn't feeling so well herself. She cooked and cleaned and tried to keep their vast porch full of knick-knacks in cobweb-free condition. She apologized for the mess.

As Mary was reeling from heartbreak at nineteen, she was coming to terms with the idea that Hayneville would forever be her home. It was a simultaneous limiting and flexing of the potential ahead: a lot of living lay in wait for her, even if it would all be in this one place. "I was young, didn't really know what I wanted to do," she said. "I always felt like this place never had enough to offer, and, at that time, I was still trying to find myself. Then again, on the spiritual side of things, I would have ended up back here anyway. Because it was in God's plan that I look after my mother; I knew that from when I was four years old. I can't explain to you how I knew that, but I knew that." She signed up for martial arts, which she loved. She had a steady job and could socialize and relish being young and attractive. She was trying not to let Mark ruin the idea of love for her, though the men that came after him were disappointments. She was in the same home as her mother and father again, in a house that her family had expanded to 2,100 square feet, with another bedroom, a big den, and a spacious hallway— luxurious for the Black side of the Black Belt. And Pattie was doing what she could to keep Mary from moving out. Walter was still at home because he needed a lot of care, but Pattie wanted her youngest daughter, who reminded her so much of her own mother, close, too.

In 1985, five years after her return, Mary took a trailer her family owned and hitched it in the grassy yard next to the house. Nearly all her siblings were out living for themselves. Enough was enough. Every grown person needed their space. She slept with a .38 semiautomatic pistol, loaded with fourteen rounds, under her pillow.

"Because people were crazy. One guy used to come to my window, girl, and talk at my window and run," she told me, by way of an explanation. Mary eventually found him out. "God showed me who he was. I didn't know who he was; God showed me," she said. "And I confronted him, and the Lord made him told on himself." She laughed saying this, still sure, after all these years, that a divine presence determined her life and saved her from its worst miseries.

Mary now knew her mother better than any of her brothers and sisters, had essentially spent more time with Pattie than all the other children. Mary would never have any children of her own. She had no tolerance for the troubles men could bring into your life. There was one guy who thought he could get away with having multiple lovers and who kept coming around her trailer years after she stopped entertaining him, but she never had time for him again. The way she had thought about marriage since she was a girl, how unfair and more difficult it was for women, probably had something to do with why she never married. And the fact that she never married had all to do with why she never had a baby. But she did, in a way, end up having a daughter: her niece, Ophelia Naomi. What a name, everyone, including me, said. One of Mary's brothers had been on drugs, and he and his girlfriend never could take care of Ophelia right. It got so bad that Mary used to sit at her desk— she was doing mortgage work at the time—and call human resources asking for advice on what to do with her brother. The state ended up taking Ophelia from her mother and giving custody of her to Mary's brother. But he was still addicted to crack, so Mary helped take over. The whole family pitched in to raise Ophelia from the time she was five, and Mary soon began to think of her as her own. She refers to Ophelia as her daughter to me and everyone else; it is as simple as that. Mary went to Parent Teacher Association meetings and combed Ophelia's hair and looked after her well-being. Ophelia introduces Mary as her "mama." She has turned out well: valedictorian of her middle school and high school, Miss Calhoun County pageant winner. Love has not ruined Mary, after all.

For women born in Alabama in the 1960s, as Mary was, men were part of how to survive. After leaving the embrace of her father, Mary had to find a man who would protect and guide her; it was as important to living as breathing in the subtropical Alabama air that took on a heaviness in summer and a sharpness in winter. Even in their activist community, the women knew their place when it came to supporting and following the lead of their men. It was supposed to be for the good of the cause. And so, women like Pattie maneuvered around the rules as best they could, deploying the power they had in the intimate relationships they worked hardest to maintain. Keeping an eye on their children, their parents and various other kin, and their lovers all at once. The whole world on their backs, it seemed like sometimes.

Tina Johnson was born in the sixties, too, and saw her mother, independent as she always was, use men to get what she wanted in life and to make up for what she would never have: a real education, a name that meant something, a cushion to fall back on when her ventures faltered or failed. The men in her life would help provide that. And it wasn't that she didn't love those men, or feel passion for nearly all of them, but she never did not need them, and so the distinction between hunger and desire was perpetually unclear. In the Black Belt, there was the double terror of being both Black and a woman: a man was needed to protect a woman both from the world and from white people. Up in the mountains of the north, a white woman didn't have to worry about anyone besides the men and women of her own kind, but that was enough.

Tina wound up not really counting James as one of her husbands: she was sixteen, and they barely spent more than a few weeks together before she left their room in his parents' house to go back to her mother's place. The entire thing lasted less than two years. He beat her up the whole time. She went to Legal Aid when she was seventeen and got a divorce; the couple had nothing to split, and she easily kept their son, Daniel. She had enough, and had the sense to see there was still an entire life ahead of her. James did not have to be it. But she had also left school, was not really working, and now had a baby on her hands. Some people, like her mother, Katherine, thought this meant that the thing she needed most was another man. Tina was barely single for a few months before she got entangled with a new one, named Randy. Katherine introduced her to him; Randy had money, and so Katherine thought they would make a good match. Randy would invite Tina and Katherine out to spend the evening at a local nightclub he owned, and he would flood their table with drinks. He always had beautiful women near him, working at the club and fussing over him, and Tina was a little impressed. She found him not without charm, but the whole thing turned out to be a mistake. Randy's family sold heroin, and Tina would have to flee that marriage as fast as she got into it. She was still a teenager.

"Girl, I was young and stupid," she recalled. "You know when you're young and think you're invincible? I was a child; I had never even drunk a beer in my life." When she finally caught on to what was happening— after her mother-in-law attacked her for talking to the police—she went back to Katherine's house for refuge.

Tina had taken care of Daniel for the first year or two of his life, but after she divorced James, she wanted to be young and go out, and her mother took on the responsibility. During Tina's time with Randy, she might get Daniel for a weekend or go see him at her mother's, but that was about it. It wasn't until she moved back in with Katherine on Sand Mountain that she took over caring for her son. She also soon met Tony. He was in medical school. They were married barely a year. He was a good man, but Tina got distracted by someone else; she would sneak off to carry on their affair. "I thought I could do anything," she said. When it came down to it, she believed she could have any man she wanted, was entitled to a certain kind of life, could get away with whatever. As long as a man wanted her. That was how her mother had lived. Tina got pregnant with her first daughter, Ashley, and decided to leave her husband. She was making a little money modeling for department stores in the county seat of Gadsden and helped out at her mother and stepfather's trucking business and grocery store. She was now with her lover, a carpenter named Earl. Sweet, but he drank too much.

During her life with Earl, Tina would unexpectedly find out that bills had gone unpaid and that things valuable to them had been pawned. She had her second daughter with him, Candelyn. But if it came down to buying a gallon of milk or a six-pack, Earl was going to buy that beer. Every day, he drank until he got drunk, usually outside in his truck after he got home from work; then he got sloppy and passed out. They lasted almost a decade before Tina became too tired, and they split up. She raised her son and daughters alone as she kept working at a grocery store and then a convenience store, until she could figure out what to do next. Earl's mother helped look after the kids while Tina was at work, and Tina saved up enough money to buy a three-bedroom cedar-sided house from her stepfather. But Katherine was always an obstacle. From the moment Tina had given birth to her son, she felt like her mother had been fighting her for him. Katherine spoiled Daniel recklessly, giving him new shoes and toys and money and the kind of affection parents can afford when they have only one child. ("He thinks the world owes him a living to this day," Tina says of Daniel now.) Katherine made moves to take Daniel permanently when he was twelve. Tina was still raising the kids alone, and exhausted from running through men. None of them was ever enough.

In the years after Earl, she dated here and there. But over the next decade, love for her wasn't the same.

Her friends teased her, asking if she was suddenly gay; they couldn't understand it. Tina still wanted men, but she had her daughters to think about now. She wasn't going to let just anyone around them. When she had a man over, she made sure her daughters were out of the house. She felt that every man was going to touch her kids, and she didn't trust any of them. It took until her girls turned four and five for Tina to realize that the sexual abuse she had experienced from her uncles was not her fault. "When I seen them, and thought, 'How could I entice that man to touch me?' They were watching TV, and I was looking at them, and it didn't register till then. I'm thinking, 'Oh my God, how could you even think that?'" she recalled. She had heard some people rationalize child abuse, say that at least the abusers didn't kill the children—but they might as well have, she thought, because it killed their minds, stopped them from becoming what they could have been. Tina believed that if she had never been touched, she probably would have done something great with her life. But she punished herself and others after the abuse finally ended. She didn't do drugs or alcohol, she just acted up. And she wondered if she had the same mania and depression her mother had, and if the abuse had made it worse. Tina would always feel like prey to men who were looking for potential victims. "They could spot me a mile off," she said. "All this been built up for all these years. And it was a dam ready to bust."

At one point, she met a wealthy older man and went out with him a few times. Katherine said she thought he was too interested in Ashley and Candelyn; Tina told her she had the wrong idea. But she watched him after that and saw that when they all had meals together, he seemed to interact with the girls a little too much. She ended the relationship. She tried not to control her daughters like Katherine had done with her, to give them the space to decide how they wanted to live. To make them see that their lives did not have to be about men and what they could get from them. But when Katherine hired a lawyer to take custody of Daniel, Tina decided not to fight it. Legal Aid told her that her mother had more resources and would likely win. Besides, Daniel wanted to go.

Tina showed up at the office of a prominent lawyer to sign custody over to her mother. Everyone in town knew him. His name was Roy Moore. She could immediately tell what kind of man he was. It was more than the way he was eying her; it was his questions about the ages of her two small girls and the color of their eyes. He wanted to know if theirs were as pretty as hers. Katherine was also watching him, but she liked how he was angling toward Tina, clearly interested. She could see his edges but also understood that he was powerful, had influence. Moore had money, must have been doing something right to be in his position. He seemed too smart not to be going somewhere even better. Katherine liked that he was hitting on Tina, and asked her to go get a drink sometime, even though Tina had told him she was happily married.

Tina already didn't want to be in that office giving up Daniel, the indignity of being near this man was too much. Later, she would wonder if he was trying to get to know her so he could know her daughters. He asked her nothing about her son, the reason she and Katherine were in his office in the first place. He wanted to get close to her girls. That's what she would come to believe. She wanted to get the hell out of there.

But when she did make her way out, behind her mother, who went out the door first, Moore grabbed her so far up her thighs, Tina felt his fingers in her vagina. One minute, she was moving through space like she had always done—not thinking, just moving—and the next minute, a stranger's hand was in the way, in her space, on her body, attacking and taking. It reminded me of the moment in class back in middle school when, as I walked down the classroom aisle to get to my desk, a boy I was friends with suddenly shot his hand up between my thighs. I was wearing jeans, but his fingers were forceful and insistent on my legs, groping me until I got past him. It was not as bad as what Tina experienced, but I felt violated all the same, embarrassed and confused. "I didn't even turn around, I just kept going," Tina recalled. "Never turned around, never told my mother. Never told her what he done, never told her nothing." All those years ago, I never turned around or told anyone, either. My classmate was popular, well liked. "She never even knew he grabbed me that day, she never knew it," Tina went on about her mother. "Now, I told other people, but I never told her. I think it's 'cause I felt like . . . 'cause she made comments about 'Well you should call him or you should do this.' I was married, and she tried to encourage me to pursue him." Tina didn't know what good it would have done to tell Katherine, so she didn't.

Things blur, fade to black. Tina couldn't remember much else from the meeting, even what happened with the custody papers. "Honestly, from the time that he was on the end of that desk, I don't remember ever 'Here, sign these papers.' I don't remember doing it," she said. All that stood out was her getting up, walking around the chairs, and his hand. "You never forget it," she said.

* * *

To be a curious teenager at the turn of the millennium in Alabama was to see there could be many ways of being in the world, and be told most of those options did not exist. The authority figures we trusted, from parents and grandparents, to teachers and pastors, and the texts we consumed, like a series of novels based on the Rapture everyone was reading, would admit there were people who had chosen alternative lifestyles, but said those people were not good or respectable, not right. Those books about the Rapture, called *Left Behind*, were inspired by the Book of Revelation and focused on nonbelievers who had been left on earth after the faithful had been raptured to heaven; the Antichrist becomes the secretary-general of the United Nations. I was vaguely scared: one lie or theft of a magazine from the grocery store, and Jesus could decide it was Judgment Day and send me to hell. We had little evidence to refute those authority figures. Despite being on TV and the internet, people who didn't conform to our socially conservative mores were mostly absent from our world. I wanted to find them. I signed up for my first America Online username in middle school and starting messaging people in chat rooms right away. My screen name was "limitedgirl14."

I knew the promise and threat of sex were online, and I was curious because I hadn't been allowed to attend sex education class and I was obsessed with the TLC album *CrazySexyCool*. I sang along and fantasized about having a man who had cheated on me. But I also wanted to connect with people who lived in different places, who knew about those alternative ways of being. Not long after I started chatting in computer lab one day, my school got a call from a local television news network. The woman with whom I had been talking—about how our days were going, what we liked to do—had called the channel after I told her where I went to school; it turned out she lived in the same place and had a similar kind of life, and she was upset that my teachers were letting me speak with potential predators on the internet. I was called into the principal's office and told to stop talking to strangers online, I was embarrassing the school.

Back then, sexuality and gender were static ideas around me. A boy was a boy, a girl was a girl, and there was nothing that was in between, or neither, or confused, or all of the above. Boys mated with girls, and any other kind of pairing was considered gross and sinful, an electric aberration best kept out of sight in case it influenced us. It seemed that a lot of people had the ability to see only what they wanted to. The sole out gay person I knew growing up was my high school chemistry teacher, who was femme and never lied about his personal life, though he never talked about it as much as some of my straight teachers did about theirs. The other adults at school seemed to accept him best that way. My classmates and I saw, but were encouraged not to look too closely.

If we did, we soon learned not to do it again. In those days, my family subscribed to a weekly newsmagazine, and I waited for its arrival on Tuesdays, so I could take it with me to read at leisure. One Tuesday afternoon, my dad was sorting through the mail when he came upon that week's issue. I watched as he picked up the magazine to take a closer look and then ripped off the cover. Before I could say anything, he handed me the magazine, the torn shards of its cover still flaring. My eyes were wide as he put the cover in the trash, and I asked him to show it to me: a loving white male couple under a headline about gay marriage. I was upset he had torn off the cover, and told him so, and my mom told him he had over-reacted. But we had to let it go. The parents of most everyone I knew felt uncomfortable with queerness, even as they talked about their all-encompassing Christian love. Gay relationships and interracial unions were better loved from afar than at home. As I grew older, my parents relaxed their stances, and they thought more liberally about queer people and read my reporting on gay rights activism. But there was no space in my life at the time to think about my gender identity, beyond the immediate discomfort I had from being seen as just a girl. The uneasiness I felt in trying to perform femininity, decades after Tina's and Mary's experiences, in a way that was just as restricting.

I watched my friends try to fit within and test the boundaries of southern white girlhood. The rules that governed how they should look and behave prized a delicateness, propriety, and innocence that were already taxing for girls who were white and came from generations of

wealth, not to mention for girls whose race kept us outside the category. I imagined it would have been easier
to be born a boy, if only to be able to move through the
world the way I wanted. Take risks, go where I wanted,
talk to whom I wanted when I wanted, cover wars if I felt
like it (which I eventually did). When I was a teenager,
the biggest fear my parents seemed to have for me was
being violated or becoming pregnant; those two fears
ruled every one of their decisions on whether I could
socialize with friends or travel on school trips. At the
same time, my parents never saw a limit to my potential.
They believed I could do anything with my life, whether
it was competing on the extemporaneous speaking circuit as part of the speech and debate team in high school
or moving to East Africa to be a foreign correspondent
at twenty-two. I roamed between femininity and mascu-
linity, using and embodying aspects of both, which felt
better and more respectable, more right, than any other
way I had thought about myself before.

But I feel a solace in Alabama that I don't feel anywhere else. It's where I always return, to relax, to think,
to breathe, from all the places I have lived over the
years—in Kampala, Lagos, and Nairobi; in Mexico City,
Los Angeles, and New York; and sometimes out of my
suitcases because I was traveling so much. In the summer of 2014, I arrived at my parents' house in Montgomery exhausted after having spent the previous four
months reporting on terrorism in northeastern Nigeria.
All I wanted to do was turn off my senses and lie in my
childhood bed. For all the horror stories set in the rural
stretches of my state, I didn't overthink pulling up to

lonely gas stations, greeting strangers in convenience stores. (That someone who looks like I do could feel that way is still somewhat novel, I know.) The trees are just the right height and span, the moss the right cool shade, the heat the right meshy weight.

The ease I feel is caught up in a sense of mystery, too. Mary would tell me something I didn't expect her to say—that she thought being dark-skinned has shaped her life as much as anything else—and I would have to reassess my assumptions all over again. In that way, Alabama is like a foreign country to me, with values I keep having to remind myself of: give thanks for your blessings, be kind to your neighbors, never forget you owe the people who came before you everything.

CHAPTER SEVEN

Alabama Neighbors

Stephanie Bryan told me she went back to Scripture when she thought about how considerate people should be. In her mind, the Poarch Creek and Alabama seem to have houses next door to each other. "We're good neighbors," she said of the tribe. She quoted the media slogan I saw on the tribe's website, under the photo of the Indian cowboy: "Alabama natives, Alabama neighbors." One of the tribe's battles is convincing state leaders that they are true and loyal citizens, not rivals or enemies, despite how ungodly they were treated in the past.

Part of Alabama's story is that, after all the awful things we've come through, are still going through, its residents are now good neighbors to a fault, trying to show that we're the opposite of our ugly stereotypes. We'll greet you on the street, welcome you inside, offer you something to drink. If I don't wave and say hello back to my parents' neighbors, including the ones with Trump signs on their front lawns, I feel like a bad neighbor. Not long ago, I was with my parents at a casual steakhouse in Montgomery, and a group of young white men came in wearing camouflage-print pants. As they walked past us, they made sure to greet my dad, who happened not to be wearing his own camouflage-print pants that day. While I was getting a Covid-19 test in a clinic outside my hometown back in 2020, I was struck by how the young white nurse ended every one of her answers to me with a gentle, deferential "ma'am." But for a long time in Alabama, being a good neighbor has meant going along to get along, prioritizing relationships over political differences, wanting to be thought of as kind when the system we inhabit is fundamentally unkind.

So, for all Stephanie's talk, she and the three thousand–odd members of the Poarch Creek are willing to be good neighbors only to a point. The tribe willed reparations, in the form of their gambling riches, to their community by force—it wouldn't have happened otherwise—but they still have to coexist with and be Alabamians, and so they have to zigzag the same way they did after surviving the Creek War and Indian removal. They want to be seen as kind, but they won't follow the rules of an unkind system.

In 2007, when Stephanie was vice chair of the tribe, it decided to build its first casino in Atmore. They gave it the airy, seductive name of "Wind Creek." The tribe was ready, Stephanie said, to "seek prosperity." They decided to open another Wind Creek casino, in Wetumpka. And then another Wind Creek casino, in Montgomery. In a move that still made some people upset, including Creek tribal members in Oklahoma, the tribe exhumed the graves of several dozen ancestors in Wetumpka to build there. The casino is at Hickory Ground, a sacred site of resistance during the Creek War and one of the Red Sticks' last significant stands. Creek prophets had blessed the soil. Warriors believed they would be immune to bullets from white men on that land, until it was too late.

"They pay everyone off," a Black Alabamian friend said to me about the tribe in the spring of 2022. We were talking about efforts in Alabama to open more avenues for gambling in addition to dog tracks. Pending bills in the most recent legislative session would have let Alabama create a gambling commission and a lottery and operate casinos and sports betting and electronic bingo, after years of legislators voting down gaming plans because they said they wanted to prevent bankruptcy, addiction, and crime. But Alabama could use the seven hundred million dollars in potential revenue. In 1999, the last time a constitutional amendment to allow a state lottery made it out of the legislature, 54 percent of voters rejected it in part because of churches' opposition to gambling. But morals were loosening as Alabamians gambled in Poarch casinos and bought lottery tickets in Georgia, Tennessee, and Louisiana, so senators kept introducing new bills with increasing support from fellow lawmakers and constituents.

The Poarch Creek have long been contending with state interference in the operation (and profits) of their casinos, from challenges to their legal authority to run them to limits on what kinds of games they can offer. Now the state was poised to become a competitor, though the tribe didn't mind. If Alabama set up a lottery and other gaming, it would hopefully leave the tribe alone. My friend wasn't sympathetic to the tribe; she also wasn't wrong about its political activities. I looked up the tribe's tax records and finished reading them not knowing much more about what the tribe believed and supported than I did when I started. In 2022, the Poarch Creek contributed $50,000 to the Common Good Fund, a liberal political action committee, and then gave $250,000 to the South Alabama Conservatives PAC two years later. In 2024, it donated around $82,000 to both the National Republican Congressional Committee and the Democratic version. (Technically, it is not the tribe giving the money, but rather its political action committees and members.) The two-sided evenness seems an attempt to be seen as neutral and inoffensive, to remain friendly with whoever is in power, is writing the story, to make sure their casinos stay open. Since 2018, the Poarch Creek have given out around $5 million to party organizations, congressional candidates, and political action committees. No amount is too much when "prosperity," as Stephanie put it, is at stake.

It is difficult to tell how much this tactic—haunting the bank accounts of the state government like ghosts of its genocidal past—is working. No one can refuse the tribe's money, but even the politicians who take it try to distance themselves. When the legislature was considering a lottery proposal in 2019, a state representative and sponsor of the bill who received contributions from the Poarch Creek told the *Montgomery Advertiser* that his intention was not to benefit the tribe; his cosponsor, who had also received donations, maintained that he "had not one conversation with the Indians about this bill." Around the same time, the *Alabama Political Reporter*, a local news outlet, claimed that the White House was investigating the tribe—Stephanie denied this—for its "monopoly in Alabama and its expansion plans." The Trump administration was watching the tribe's activities in the state legislature around the lottery and gaming proposals, the article said, and it quoted a "former White House insider" who said that Trump had a "disdain for Indian underhanded tactics" and that "what the tribe is up to in Alabama is being heard in Washington." The racist message came through clearly: the Poarch Creek are untrustworthy. The article went on to say that the tribal council and its lobbyists were "harassing" members of the legislature. "I took their money," one lawmaker was quoted as saying. "But I didn't promise to give them the state in return."

It wasn't meant to be like this. Stephanie became the first female chair of the tribe in 2014. "But we are a matrilineal society," she quickly reminded me. "History shows that the women were the strong leaders in our tribe." At the time of her election, Stephanie made sure to visit state legislators and city and county officials and tell them she wanted to work together, that the Poarch Creek wanted to help them make their state a better one. She told the governor, a bullish conservative woman named Kay Ivey, that she had children and grandchildren living in Alabama and that she wanted them to feel good about where they came from. The way Stephanie tells it, she refuses to understand why the tribe and the state have to be on opposite sides—they can disagree, but that doesn't change the fact that Stephanie and the tribe are also constituents of Alabama. The state government has no business behaving out of fear because of the tribe's success. "We've paid millions of dollars in payroll taxes and millions of dollars in cost of goods throughout the state, so the economic impact we've had on the state has been very successful for the state," she said. "People should be proud of us." She believes that when people outside the tribe take the time to get to know its members, they see how caring and kind they are: "That's why we were called the Friendly Creeks." Not quite the reason, but we all interpret history the way we need to for survival.

Stephanie tells whoever asks that she could never have imagined becoming the tribe's first female chairman and chief executive officer, but she spent much of her career laboring for the Poarch Creek. She put in time working for the tribe's job training program and then at its police station and for its social services program, all of which were funded by federal grants. She helped write an application for a grant that would give the Poarch Creek assistance to pay for childcare so that parents could go to work or school. Later still, she moved to its housing department, helping solicit a grant to improve members' homes. There were elders who had houses where Stephanie could see the dirt ground below the slats in the floor. After she married and had children, she called herself a stay-at-home mom, but she never stopped working. She ran a day care center out of her living room so she could make money while being close to her kids. "I done that for years," she said. When her kids grew older, she went into insurance, convincing people to take out life policies so their families would be protected should anything happen to them. Now she could frame that trajectory as a journey of wanting to help people.

She often traveled to Washington, D.C., to lobby on behalf of the tribe and Indian country. When she gave speeches at places like the Junior League of Montgomery or the Birmingham Rotary Club, she spoke with a sense of surprise about being a poor Indian girl who had somehow made it to a place of power. Whenever she was in D.C., she joked in her disarming drawl that she was proudly from "L.A."—not the metropolis, but "Lower Alabama." Several years before we met, she sat with former president Barack Obama at a luncheon. The tribe was building a twenty-million-dollar Boys and Girls Club in Alabama at the time. That day, she told Obama that she never could have imagined herself being at a table to ask the president to protect Indian country. She remembered him responding that they had both made history, because he had never expected to be president, either. Stephanie cried at the luncheon—she still has the photos showing it—but they were tears of happiness, of disbelief at what the tribe had overcome. In one photo, she is embracing Obama, looking at the leader of her country with emotional intensity. As the leader of her other country, she wanted to diversify its businesses to be more than just another tribe getting rich off casinos. The Poarch Creek were now buying hotels, like four they acquired with an investment group near Disney World.

That the state of Alabama sees the tribe as more

threatening than good is something that Stephanie will have to continue to mitigate. Dealing with politicians involves giving them a history lesson every time she sees them: why the tribe is sovereign, why it needs its own government, what its members have been through. Talking about it can make her emotional. When we spoke, her voice got shaky.

Stephanie felt that she treated everybody the same, with respect, no matter their color or background, but the same was not afforded to the tribe. Her grandmother, who told Stephanie never to be ashamed of her Native heritage, had barely gone to school, and it was some wonder that the tribe, by 2019, had already given a generation of college students fifty thousand dollars each to put toward their education, and would keep doing so for enrolled members.

Her job was not easy, Stephanie told me. There were mornings when she woke up wondering why she had chosen to do it. It made her think back to when she ran for Poarch Creek Princess, another title she had not been sure she wanted. But her ambition had led her to both places. From going to get her teeth cleaned in an Airstream to overseeing the construction of a seventy-thousand-square-foot health clinic with top-quality medical and lab services.

In many regards, the tribe has the right advantages this round. Stephanie and many of the other leaders can pass as white. Stephanie has gone from the girl with a puff of dark hair and tribal headdress crowned Poarch Creek Princess to the woman with a soft demeanor masking an extraordinarily tough outlook. The rez is a whole new place, more modern, more of a home for its elders than it ever has been. Dirt roads and beaten-up school buses now belong to tribal oral history. The Poarch Creek have Alabamian accents, Alabamian values. They love family, God, football, and, like any good Christian, "everybody" around them. Their new money is the most salient result of their decades of hardship and struggle, but not nearly the only important one.

"The constant fight for our sovereignty is a challenge daily," Stephanie said. Even as she was being elected chief, the tribe was fighting multiple lawsuits. The state tax assessor was suing the Poarch Creek for the right to tax their property, challenging its federally protected status; the Muscogee Nation was suing because the tribe had built the casino on Hickory Ground, reburying or storing elsewhere the human remains and artifacts, and they wanted the casino destroyed and the grave site restored; and the state attorney general was trying to ban slot machine gambling at their casinos, claiming in the suit it was a "public nuisance." (For what it's worth, the former mayor of Atmore, Jim Staff, once said of the tribe's casinos, "It aggravates me every time people start on that. People are going to spend their money on what they want to do. That's sovereign property out there. It doesn't belong to the state of Alabama. It's really helping people around here. We like the jobs. They are good paying jobs.")

The tribe has its own story, too. Its founding myth propels the Indian nation just as Alabama's does, justifying whatever has to be done to create and solidify its borders. In the case of the Poarch Creek, the events are so recent, the tribe still has a hangover from the tumultuous time.

The story goes like this: Some six decades ago, Stephanie's people were a tribe, and they had fought and scraped every limb to stay together. But they had to prove it. With treaties, federal censuses, land receipts, whatever they had. The federal government required that any tribe that wanted sovereignty had to show evidence that it had been a distinct entity since the start of the twentieth century, an island unto itself, and that it had political domain over its members. And those members had to genetically belong to the tribe—through blood quantum tests, tribal rolls, census records, and other methods that would supposedly measure racial affiliation. This belonging, in the eyes of the U.S. government, was essentially all the wealth they had. In the early 1940s, an American ethnologist named Frank Speck visited the Poarch Creek. When he encountered the Indians, Speck wrote, the group was living in the shadow of Jim Crow and deepening class stratification in the state. No other contemporary Indian tribe had come closer to social extinction than these Creek living east of the Mississippi. Just a dozen or so elders had given way to a group of people who had succeeded in staying put near a tiny railroad station named Poarch despite the best efforts of Alabama to make them join the Trail of Tears through the 1830s and '40s. Come the 1940s, the tribe had yet to find a leader who could secure for them a better life, Speck observed.

But beginning in the 1960s, the Poarch Creek were one of dozens of native peoples who saw their last chance to get what was owed to them: the will to decide their own futures. Most of their old land was lost forever, but at least they had this. Tribes the size of the Poarch Creek were agitating around the country for federal recognition. The established "Five Tribes"—the Cherokee, Chickasaw, Choctaw, Creek, and Seminole—had dominated the arena of relations between the federal government and Indian country and wanted a say in which contending tribes could join them. The Five Tribes helped create an exacting, evidence-based process that would confer legitimacy, one designed to exclude any group seen as unqualified or undesirable, especially since most of the unofficial tribes claimed kinship to them. The Poarch Creek banded together to fund-raise for their chief's lobbying trips to Washington, D.C., where he met with politicians to gain support for recognition.

Chief Calvin McGhee was a dirt-poor farmer, but he had fought for the Poarch Creek for most of his adult life. In 1950, he organized thousands of Creek into the Creek Nation East of the Mississippi; the tribe elected him as permanent chairman in 1951, in recognition of his service. He cut a glorious figure: ruddy skin, reddish-brown hair, and blue eyes beneath a red-and-white-feathered headdress he put on to meet elected officials, like President John F. Kennedy. (He told JFK, Mark Edwin Miller writes in *Claiming Tribal Identity*, that his people had helped Andrew Jackson during the Indian wars down south. Friendly to the end.) Chief Calvin started up communication with other tribes in Indian country and set about reviving their cultural rituals: powwow dancing, the making and wearing of traditional dress. And he was strategic: he deployed his feathered and beaded regalia as both a celebration of his people and an emotional appeal to white lawmakers that evoked the nostalgic place of Indians in the public imagination. Humble farmer and savvy politician. Indian agitator and southern gentleman.

In 1962, on behalf of the Poarch and other Creek descendants in the Southeast, Chief Calvin sued the federal government for payment for the land it had seized from the Creek in 1814. He won that fight, and the Indian Claims Commission awarded almost $4 million to Creek groups in both the Southeast and Oklahoma; the money was paid to them about a decade later. Taking out legal fees and other expenses, each Creek ended up being entitled to $112.13. The claims commission was a shaky setup, created by Congress after World War II out of guilt for how tribes had been exploited and displaced, and out of gratitude for the Indians who had served their country anyway. But the commission was exploitative, too: some tribes had to agree to permanently give up their claims to federal recognition if they wanted to be compensated for lost land. It took thirty years for most of the claims to be paid out.

The tribe had its own ways to fund-raise money so it could send Chief Calvin to Washington as cheaply and as often as possible. Stephanie described those afternoons in a phrase: "the cook and the chicken and the washpot." The women battered chicken and dropped it into hot grease and then used sticks to stir it so the pieces wouldn't stick together. As the adults shooed her away from the pot of bubbling chicken and grease, Stephanie could sense the crack of urgency in the air, the feeling that everything depended on this. After the chicken was crisply fried and giving off a smell so thick and sweet it could almost make a person sick, they portioned it off into individual "chicken dinners" for sale. The washpot was stored at her aunt Marie's house.

Chief Calvin died in 1970, unable to see the results of all his troubles when the tribe was finally recognized in 1984. The Poarch Creek would become the only federally recognized tribe in Alabama, one of three Indian tribes recognized in the Southeast, and the only recognized one east of the Mississippi. The U.S. government designated around 230 acres of land as their reservation. From 21 million acres ceded to the American union, much of it to the nascent creation now known as Alabama, in 1814 down to 230 acres returned in 1985. Still, the land is theirs.

Alabama neighbors. When the tribe built the first Wind Creek casino, a local textile mill was going out of business, putting some one thousand people out of work because their jobs were going overseas, as Stephanie remembered. The casino gave those people, a lot of them women, employment opportunities. The tribe had no plans to stop. It was buying hotels and entertainment venues throughout the country, running two racetracks in Alabama and Florida, and had acquired a $1.3 billion casino in Pennsylvania and two gaming resorts in Aruba and Curaçao. The tribe was small enough that it could make sure the next generation was taken care of. But it let its tribal fire and police stations serve all the residents of Escambia County, not just members on the rez, and their Boys and Girls Club served every interested kid. Every year, the tribe also gave millions of dollars to charities around the state, Stephanie said, and paid its employees a good living wage. All this makes for a great case: the tribe was fucked over, there is no doubt of it, and yet it is somehow not angry—as long as no one gets in the way of what it is due. I appreciate the ruthlessness; it is another very Alabamian thing about the Poarch Creek.

"It may always be an antagonistic relationship—I don't know—but it's not for lack of us trying to mend whatever bridges that were broken," Stephanie told me. "I believe in sitting down face-to-face: 'What is the problem, what can we do to compromise to solve the problem?'" The Poarch Creek don't believe they are asking for much; Alabama could at least give them the courtesy of working together. But that is the crux of the state's misgivings: if they do and Alabama advances, so will the tribe. Stephanie was sure they would do so, regardless. "I am a visionary," she said simply and seriously. "And God has blessed me with great strategic and analytical skills." She read books on leadership by pastor and motivational speaker John C. Maxwell. "We are the first Americans," she said. That part of the story is another thing owed the Poarch Creek, in Alabama's textbooks and museums, in its statues and parks. The first Alabamians. Nobody else can say that.

CHAPTER EIGHT

New Arrivals

What about the people who arrived after the Alabamians who left? My dad got here first, after going to flight school in Northern California in 1976 and then leaving for Alabama about two years later, when he no longer wanted to be a pilot. My mom arrived soon after. My grandmother had raised my dad and his brothers and sister alone in Lagos; when she proudly sent him, the eldest son, abroad, they both expected he would return at some point. My mom's brother-in-law managed a TV station in Lagos, and he had promised her a job as a news anchor when she returned. "You belong on TV!" he told her. She had interned at the station during summers and came to Alabama to study broadcasting. Both my parents had attended Catholic boarding schools before moving, and though my dad had grown up without enough money, they were not fleeing poverty or conflict. They intended to go back to Nigeria.

Alabama was a bucolic Ellis Island. I suppose its Statute of Liberty would have been the grass-green sign on I-65 near the border with Tennessee that, since 2003, has read "Welcome to Sweet Home Alabama"; before that, it said "Alabama the Beautiful." About a mile south is an Alabama Welcome Center, which has a truck stop and a long, low building with staff who are there to give out calendars, maps, and tourist brochures of "thousands of destinations, attractions, accommodations and events," but who mostly give travelers directions and point them to the bathrooms. Whenever we drove long distances on an interstate, I begged my parents to stop at the centers so I could raid the vending machines. They usually said no. They weren't new to town anymore. They had become citizens thanks to the last time the country agreed to expansive immigration reform.

The Voting Rights Act of 1965 outlawed the voting obstacles put into law after slavery: literacy tests and poll taxes and property requirements. It did nothing about the greatest obstacle of all, the violence, but at least the ground at the polls became legally smooth. Two months after the Voting Rights Act passed came the Immigration and Nationality Act; President Lyndon B. Johnson signed it into law. A close adviser of Johnson's said the president "eventually recognized that existing immigration law, and in particular, national origins quotas created many decades before on racist grounds, as inconsistent with civil rights and racial justice." The Voting Rights

Act transformed the lives of Black people who wanted to be treated like citizens in the Deep South, and the Immigration Act transformed the lives of people who wanted to try living in the Deep South, like my parents. The Immigration Act got rid of quotas based on national origin and intended to reunite people with relatives here and lure skilled workers. It was devised and enacted with the energy of the civil rights movement in mind.

The federal government had created quotas in the 1920s to keep immigration confined to Europeans, at a time when eugenics and its theories of white Anglo-Saxon genetic superiority pervaded social policy. It gave out a maximum of 150,000 visas a year according to the nationality quotas, which were calculated from the 1920 Census. The more people of a given nationality already present in the United States, the more likely people of that nationality could come join them. But the government kept out Black Americans from the quota calculations. It classified white Americans and immigrants according to their nation of origin and Black Americans and immigrants by race, meaning that no African nationalities had immigration allowances. Africans could not enter the United States. Based on the quotas, immigrants from Asia, the Middle East, and even southern and eastern Europe also found it almost impossible to get in.

The revised system set up a scheme that favored immigrants who already had family in the United States who were citizens or permanent residents and allowed for admission based on desired labor skills, too. Soon enough, arrivals from other countries, especially those coming out from under colonial rule, surged. Ambitious people of various colors decided that this nation would be another home. Nigeria won its independence on October 1, 1960, after nearly a century of British rule. On Tafawa Balewa Square in the island city of Lagos, then the capital, a flag with thick green and white stripes rose to replace the British Union Jack, and fireworks blew up the sky. Soon, its young and bright would be leaving for the United States or Europe or the former Soviet Union—not for the rest of their lives, but for enough time to get a good education and see the world as Nigeria built its institutions, so they could return to help remake their country. That was the plan.

Alabama State University would seem an unlikely place for my parents to attend and then meet. The college, one of the country's oldest Historically Black Universities, began operating in a town called Marion in 1867, in central Alabama's Perry County, and was initially called the Lincoln Normal School. After the Civil War, nine free Black people had pooled together five hundred dollars, the story goes, to create a place for Black Alabamians to learn. With the aid of the American Missionary Association and the Freedmen's Bureau, those free Black men and others created a curriculum that would provide a classical education in math, Greek, chemistry, and history and, eventually, train teachers. The school, one of the first established for Black Americans after the war ended, went through trial after trial: a fire that could have been arson by white residents in town; a lack of funding and general neglect from the state; a loss of income from tuition during the Great Depression. For a time, teachers agreed to go without salaries if supporters of the school provided them with food; students and townspeople raised funds for the school to keep it going. Its teacher training division spun off into ASU, first known as the Alabama State College for Negroes, in Montgomery.

But it survived. By the late 1920s, the Lincoln Normal School had almost six hundred students and thirty teachers, eleven buildings on a forty-acre campus, two dormitories for students, and a working farm. Nineteen sixty-seven marked the one-hundredth anniversary of its opening, and in 1969, its final high school class graduated. The next year, the school closed after Perry County began integrating its public schools. But its alumni association held on to one of the campus buildings and bought part of the original twenty-two acres. The land is still in their hands.

If you look at one of the black-and-white photos from the marches that Martin Luther King Jr. led from Selma to Montgomery in March 1965, there is a young Black man at the end of the front row of protestors, his arm linked with the arms of other men and women going all the way down to Dr. King, solemn in a black suit. The young man might have been one of the most casually dressed marchers there that day: he is wearing an Alabama State T-shirt. Before the hundreds of protestors reached the City of St. Jude Catholic Church on Fairview Avenue in Montgomery, some eight hundred other Alabama State students joined them as the march continued to the steps of the state capitol. Much like how Mary McDonald's parents were putting up civil rights activists over in Lowndes

County, and her family's neighbors were registering people to vote and running mutual aid societies, the students
and professors at Alabama State were at the center of the
capital city's resistance. It's a thread that grounds Alabama's civil rights fairy tale, one that locals and outsiders
alike tend not to know. There is another black-and-white
photo, this time of four young Black men, Alabama State
students who had just been expelled from the college
for staging a sit-in with twenty-one other students at the
Montgomery County Courthouse on February 25, 1960,
to protest Jim Crow laws. The students had been inspired
by sit-ins earlier that month at lunch counters in Greensboro and Nashville. For weeks, they had met at Black
churches so they could plan and get the word out. In the
photo, the four men are wearing slim, elegant coats and
look aggrieved, but defiant.

In the 1940s, when a young Black man from Selma
named F. D. Reese was studying for a degree in science,
his teachers at Alabama State encouraged him to think
independently about the matter of civil rights. After grad-
uating, Reese would invite Dr. King to come work with
voting activists in his hometown, which eventually led to
the Selma-to-Montgomery marches. In 1955, an Alabama
State professor named Jo Ann Robinson used a college
mimeograph machine to help make thousands of flyers
urging her students and colleagues, and people throughout the city, to stay off buses on the day of Rosa Parks's
trial. That action would lead to the Montgomery Bus Boycott. Not long after she moved to the city six years earlier,
Robinson had herself been harassed by a bus driver for
sitting in the whites-only section of a bus. An Alabama

State student, Vera Harris, helped pass out those flyers. Harris and her husband would later open their
home to Freedom Riders. Fred Gray, another Alabama
State graduate, strategized with Robinson about the
bus boycott in her living room. He defended Parks in
court and went on to file a federal lawsuit that pushed
state officials to allow the Selma-to-Montgomery
marches to proceed. And after Alabama State expelled
nine students for that courthouse sit-in because of pressure from the governor, in 1960, Gray defended the students and had them reinstated.

As my mom, Regina, was preparing to graduate from high school in Benin City, Nigeria, my
grandfather asked her what she wanted to do next. He
hadn't gone to much school, but he valued education
greatly. He was a self-made man who had built a successful transportation business and wanted the best for all his
children. (His friends had even come around the house to
comment, "You're sending all your girls to America? Why?
It's the boys that need to go to school.") My aunt Rosemary
was already studying at Alabama A&M University, in
Huntsville, and my mom eventually decided she wanted
to go to the United States, too. She had first imagined she
would go to the University of Ibadan, in the churning
southern Nigerian city where she had spent much of her
childhood, but my grandfather told her to give America
a chance; she could always return if she didn't like it. My
mom began applying to schools the next year.

"A lot of my friends were already saying, 'Don't go to
the South!' And I said, 'Well, I want to be closer to Rosemary, to where she is.' They said, 'Don't go to the South,

because they have the KKK.' They were trying to scare me," my mom recalled. "Alabama had a bad reputation, even in Nigeria in those old, old days." Another of her sisters, Susan, took heed of the warnings and decided to go to college in Oklahoma. My mom applied to a number of schools, but Alabama State ended up being the most straightforward path; the head of international student affairs at the time was kind and helpful, facilitating her paperwork at the U.S. embassy.

My mom knew about the Ku Klux Klan, but there were so many other things she didn't know. For one, she had no idea that Alabama State was a Historically Black institution. "I did not know ASU was a Black school, because the director of international student affairs was a white man! And we didn't have internet," she told me in her defense.

My mom was nineteen, going on twenty, when she arrived in Alabama in the summer of 1978. Having grown up the fifth-oldest of fourteen brothers and sisters, with her father, her mother, and her father's other wife, it was a novel thing to be on her own in a place where she knew no one. She had unwittingly arrived in Montgomery at the tail end of a school holiday. The office for international students put her in touch with another Nigerian woman, whose apartment she stayed in until the dorms opened again in a few days. Her arrival on that holiday didn't feel like an auspicious start. Her sister hadn't even picked her up at the airport. She wanted to send her father a telegram saying she wasn't sure Alabama was a good idea. Still, she stayed. She gave her host chin chin, a crunchy fried dough treat that her mom had sent along with her, and prepared herself for the day school reopened.

But she never became comfortable at Alabama State. My mom had always liked to sit up front in class and raise her hand to answer as many questions as she could; when she did that at her new school, other students asked her who she thought she was and pretended not to understand her accent. People liked to ask her, with real but insensitive curiosity, "Why are you here?" To give you a sense of the kind of person my mom is, some people would even ask her, "Why are you so happy all the time?" She started to sit toward the back of her classes. Her roommate barely greeted her, and the girls in the dorm never invited her out. She could barely eat the food: "They said, 'You want a hot dog?' I said, 'What hot dog? You killed the dog? What is in it?'" my mom recalled.

It was an unexpected relief to have the tiny circle of Nigerian students around. A woman at the American embassy had told her there would be Nigerians at Alabama State, but my mom was unsure if she would get along with them. She ended up eating jollof rice and plantain with them, going to the dance parties they threw, and, soon enough, seeing my dad in the college library. She kept her room in the dorm, but ended up spending much of her time at his apartment. While she found Black Alabamians her age mostly unwelcoming, her fellow new Alabamians felt like home.

"It helped tremendously," my mother said, thinking back. "Having that Nigerian community." They must have numbered less than thirty, but it was enough. One man, still a beloved family friend to this day, gleefully called out "Reggie, baby!" whenever he saw her on campus. Another friend, who had ethnic scarification on his face, made the whole circle laugh when he told them an American student had asked him if he got the scars while fighting a lion. He had responded, "Yes, I did."

My mom stayed In Alabama for just a year. She transferred to the University of Tennessee when she followed my dad there for his graduate program. She had no plans to come back, no desire to.

Before my mom even arrived in Alabama, my dad, David, was attending college classes in Berkeley but was unsure of how to continue paying the expensive tuition. One day, he went to a library to look at a directory of universities around the country. "I didn't realize there were schools dedicated just for Black people," he told me. "So, I saw Alabama State—that was the number one school listed because it was alphabetical—and that's the only school that I applied for. I thought, 'I have to experience this.'" Unlike my mother, he knew what he was getting into. Alabama had race issues, but which state didn't?

As with my mom, the director of international student affairs helped my dad through the enrollment process. He studied for a degree in economics, but realized he was enjoying his communications classes. He wrote for the campus newspaper, which he also liked. It was all a nice surprise. He lived on campus for a time and then decided to move off; many Nigerians lived in apartments downtown. They saw one another often and gave each other rides when needed. "Those are the things that make you feel like home. It's like you're still back in

Nigeria, but you're in the United States," my dad said. "So, you're getting the best of both worlds." He had a yellow Volkswagen Bug that he zipped around Montgomery in; once, he did see some KKK members gathered on the Southern Bypass, which runs through the city, for a parade. He calmly passed them, but was shocked to see them marching in the crystaline sunlight.

Despite their difficulties blending in, my parents were cool. The visual evidence is in the thick photo albums they keep in our family home. My dad wore silky shirts unbuttoned halfway down his chest, tight pants, and rainbow-striped suspenders over white T-shirts with bell-bottom jeans; he had a stylishly bushy Afro. My mom was in leather and satin pants, slim corduroy blazers, and the same rainbow-striped suspenders over black turtlenecks with jeans and heels. They loved wearing giant sunglasses and vests with matching trousers. In one photo, my dad is in a rust-colored leather jacket while intently reading *Ebony* magazine. Together they seemed to be up for most anything; now was the time to choose the kind of people they wanted to be, the kind of lives they wanted to lead, even if it was in this strange state.

My dad was curious about cigarettes, so he tried smoking them for a while. Later on, he smoked a pipe because he was in graduate school to become a professor and had read in novels that professors smoked pipes, so he wanted to try that, too. He got into jazz, which my mom could do without, and they both danced to Michael Jackson and Smokey Robinson and Stevie Wonder. They went to see *Grease* at a drive-in theater, a movie my father loved so much that he bought a VHS copy that I would watch over and over as a kid. Stacks of my mom's sordid romance novels survived the decades to reach our family garage in the early 2000s; she hungrily read pages of Jackie Collins while she cooked.

At school, my dad found some Black students friendly toward him, and he endeared himself by being generous with his time and knowledge when classmates needed help with lessons. He dated a few American girls. Still, it was difficult to socialize and be at ease with Black Alabamians. "What I found is that African Americans are just as naïve about us," my dad told me, "as we are about them. Even though we are similar in color, we didn't have much in common." My dad had thought it would be easy to fit in at this all-Black school, that he would be readily accepted. Instead, no one made much of an effort to get to know him, to help him settle into a world where he was only starting to pick up the customs. Mostly what he felt was indifference. "It could be because they were not aware we needed some accommodation from them for us to feel welcome," he recalled. "We faced similar struggles, yet were dealing with the problems differently because of our cultural backgrounds." But he would soon find his people: other Nigerians, and Kenyans, and an Ethiopian who had somehow ended up in Alabama, too. It was a matter of survival and hedonism. They did well in their classes, commiserated about their professors and other students, and went to nightclubs.

My dad ended up enjoying his time at Alabama State. With his transferred credits, he would spend just shy of two years at the university. When he graduated near the top of his class, he decided he would go on to get a Ph.D.

in journalism at the University of Tennessee. With my mom, now his fiancée, right with him, he moved to Knoxville. He was not sure if he would ever return to Alabama.

He had started thinking about being a college professor. He loved learning new things, loved reading books, loved studying and writing papers. School was an environment in which he had thrived since he was small. While he was completing his doctorate, my dad ran into the former chair of the communications department at Alabama State; she was just starting her doctorate in journalism at Tennessee and wondered if he would be interested in applying for her old job at his alma mater. After he graduated, he was offered the job of assistant professor and head of the entire department. After some deliberation with my mom, he decided to take the job. "I was anxious to kind of go home," he recalled. "I still had some of my former classmates, my friends, living here; we kept in contact. And I really did enjoy my time here." My parents had been visiting Montgomery every so often since leaving for Tennessee, coming to see their friends over the weekends. He knew how his old college worked.

But his circumstances had changed. "One of the things that I never realized as a student, but that I came to realize as an adult, is that a lot of African Americans tend to see Africans as competitors—they think we're here to take their jobs, they think we're here to take opportunities that are set aside for them, they think we're not really Black," my dad told me. "Which is really unfortunate because, essentially, we are all the same, facing the same social and economic challenges. African Americans remain and will always be my people." He took a minute, thought some more. "But when I came back, I was able to get a bet-ter understanding of how ASU fit into the society itself. I never figured it out as a student," he said. "ASU has really been a fighter in the civil rights movement. Whatever mis-givings I have about my experience at ASU, I have a lot of respect for the institution." He stayed at Alabama State until 2017, when he retired; a year later, he returned to teaching journalism at another university in Montgomery.

Alabama State's battles continued. In 1981, John F. Knight Jr., later the school's executive vice president and chief operating officer, co-filed a federal lawsuit against the state over the school's decades-long struggle to stay open. Among other things, the suit argued that the state property tax structure was biased against Black Alabam-ians and had forced the public university to operate with severely underfunded programs. The devisers of the tax code in the 1901 constitution had pushed for mini-mal taxation of their property, which was later amplified through amendments that deprived Black public school students. The destitute education system resulted in fail-ing schools for all publicly educated students, Black and white. Collateral damage for the cause. Over thirty years later, a federal court found that Alabama's property tax laws did in fact discriminate against Black people, but it ruled that the plaintiffs had not proven that the laws causing the K–12 public school system to be insufficiently funded were segregating the experiences of higher edu-cation in the state, or negatively affecting the ability of Black students to attend college.

I grew up on the ASU campus. After my dad picked me up from school, he often deposited me in the library in his building, where the librarians let me hunt for and sit with things I wanted to read, before I eventually made my way to the computer lab, where I'd seize an empty station to get on the internet. I roamed the faculty offices in the communications department, making friends with my dad's colleagues and students, going barefoot on the worn carpet. One summer, I was in a science program on campus with other Black high school students I made friends with, had crushes on. It enhanced my sense of self, I see now, to be surrounded by Black scholars in a setting of unselfconscious Blackness. I felt more belonging there than either of my parents ever had. Their story of coming to Alabama State had turned again.

CHAPTER NINE

Newer Arrivals

Other foreigners made their way to Alabama, too. By 1989, seven out of ten farmworkers in the Southeast were foreign. Most of them were Mexican. Mexicans had been picking cotton seasonally in the South since just after the turn of the twentieth century, many in Mississippi and Louisiana and Arkansas. They picked in the fall and left by the winter, though some stayed to work as sharecroppers year-round. By 2000, Mexicans were arriving in rural and small-town Alabama to join a market hungry for workers in its poultry- and meat-processing factories and forestry industry. From 2000 to 2010, the Latino population in Alabama grew 145 percent—faster than in every other state but South Carolina. White planters welcomed them onto their fruit and vegetable farms, complaining that they had no one to work their fields once Black people started leaving them.

Brandon Vela was in elementary school and in the fields. He had heard plenty of horror stories from people who were mistreated while they picked, were rushed, had very short or no breaks, and had no room to leave— they needed the money too badly. Brandon's mother wouldn't tolerate those conditions, even though they needed the money badly, too, and she was ready to move if troubles arose. But mostly, their bosses showed up right when the work was done for the day, and were not overly strict, meaning the faster Brandon and the other workers picked, the sooner they could go home. This meant putting their bodies into overdrive, sneaking protein and candy bars to eat in the field. Brandon's mom sometimes made small burritos in the morning, and they ate them before their shifts.

But whether your boss is decent or bad, the labor is the same. So is the heat. After a while, your skin starts to look fried. Everybody has patches of dry and sensitive boils, sweats excessively, and gets the chills from dehydration. But the picking has to be done. Working on small-scale farms, about two hundred or so acres in size, means adapting to the myriad needs of Alabama's fruits and vegetables. Picking each crop requires unique skills and armor, and each crop has different effects on the body.

A commonly grown crop in Alabama is the peach, which usually flowers, fuzzy and round and bright, on trees around six to nine feet high. You stand in tall, heavy boots, with jeans and socks tucked inside, in a field of high grass wet from mildew, arch back your neck, and look up into the trees, which means you need sunglasses to see through the light. The sunglasses also protect you

from falling insects and dry leaves and branches when
you reach for the fruit; it is impossible to know what is
lurking up there. A large-brimmed hat is also necessary to
avoid as much of the direct sun as possible. The wise put
bandannas around their faces, too, covering their noses
and reaching back to their ears, to avoid wayward peach
fuzz, which has been known to cause sneezing, coughing,
and itching, like a bad cold or allergy. Best not breathed in.
With all these items on, you are now more protected from
threats, including snakes nesting in the green, but you are
also more uncomfortable—it is likely at least ninety-five
degrees Fahrenheit outside and only getting hotter. The
trees seem to prevent the circulation of air and, instead,
push a thick steam into your pores. In the afternoon, you
change out of your boots, which are helpful in keeping
out moisture and preventing foot fungus, and into lighter
sneakers.

The men and women and children in their long sleeves
are absorbing so much heat that it can start to feel like a
red haze that will not let up. There is no shade out on the
fields, because it would be bad for the crops. The hours
tend to be from six in the morning until about noon, when
it gets too hot out. Sometimes five thirty in the morning
until two in the afternoon, if their bodies can make it. All
the while, each part of your body is covered and snug,
but also suffocating and wilting. Every moment begins to
feel like it should be your last of the day in the green, but
there are still more to come.

Brandon wondered if the pain of the labor was compa-
rable to the times his mom gave birth; she often said that
her body ached from picking, and she sometimes had a

burning sensation in the place where her stomach was cut open for two C-sections.

Every job is different. Brandon picked blueberries for a long time. They sprout, small and bursting and dark, on bushes that are about eight feet tall, not too bad, kind of shaped like big shrubs with flexible limbs that he could pull down to reach the fruit. You make sure to wear jeans you can throw out at the end of the season, because stains are inevitable: berry stains, grass stains, mud stains. But at least he could stand up.

There are other crops—like tomatoes, squash, and cucumbers—that grow along the ground, force you to spend most of the day bent over. It would be six in the morning when Brandon pulled up to the fields to begin a shift picking something like tomatoes or squash, and the dread he felt was almost physical. Only about thirty minutes of moving along the rows of crop would pass before his back started screaming at him to stand up and take a break. He stood, readjusted, and started again. He wore a back brace. The job was literally backbreaking, Brandon thought.

Most of the people out in the field with him weren't young enough to be doing this kind of work. Many of them were middle-aged, some in their sixties. He couldn't imagine the stress on their bodies. Nobody complained, though. Instead, they talked about their lives, about recipes, about trips to the beach. They became friends. Brandon believed it had to do with their mindset. Where else were they going to go? What else were they going to do? They had to give it all they had, ignore the pain, push through. It was a beautiful mindset, he thought, to be

strong like that—but it didn't stop their bodies from taking in the damage. Whenever he worked with his mom,
he frequently stood up and held his back, and his mom
just kept picking and picking. She occasionally stood
when Brandon did and asked him if he was okay; he
usually told her he was tired. She often told him to take
a deep breath, not think about it for too long, stretch, and
get back to it. It does something to you, being constantly
bent over like that. To be the most productive, you have
to stay hunched. It helped him to stay bent if he counted
the time in ten-minute intervals.

Potatoes also grow on the ground. Knees down, hands
in the mush. You can't just pull them out: you have to wig-
gle your hands to unearth the submerged parts. Stretchy
clothes are ideal; gloves are pointless, they will fill with
dirt as soon as you put them into the soil. When Brandon
was kneeling with the potatoes, he could shimmy down
a row of them, rooting around and filling his bucket, and
the position was better on his back. At the end, his nails
were packed with dirt and chipped by rocks. You should
clean them, but know that the same thing will happen
tomorrow.

The labor requires care, delicacy. Red tomatoes can't
be picked if green ones are demanded. The fruit can't be
gripped too tightly or squeezed. The mounds of produce
have to look presentable. This is the daily routine, Brandon said, this is the daily life.

* * *

But for Brandon, thank God, not anymore. The thing
about being a good neighbor in Alabama is that it

increasingly requires you to agree with your neighbor in order to be in harmony, at least in this political era, and to accept the intolerable reality that your neighbors may be kind to you as an individual but hostile to the group to which you belong. Brandon exemplifies more than most what it means to be a good neighbor; he also sees more than the rest how that will still not make the arrangement fairer. But like Alabamians before him, that doesn't stop him from trying.

Brandon's been zigzagging across the map of legitimacy since he was born in another country by mistake. He was twenty at the time we met in 2018. When his parents left Mexico for the United States they were around the same age, with him as a baby in tow. But that was the second time they left. The first time his parents left Mexico, they were traveling with a small child, Brandon's older brother, and his mother Olivia was pregnant with him. But they had such difficulty navigating the American health care system with no English or money or way to get around that they felt they had to return to their native country for her to deliver. Friends and family often said they wished Olivia had just stayed, so Brandon could have been an American citizen. "I just think, 'Bless her heart, that is a huge decision, and what can you do?'" Brandon said. "I don't blame her whatsoever, and I feel grateful that we are tied together, because I guess essentially we're kind of all the same, we're from the same place, we're from the same heritage."

It is a shame, though. His story could have been a lot like mine. From the stories his mom and dad told him, Brandon felt like his parents had lived in something like the Stone Age during their childhoods in rural Mexico: homes were basic, electricity was rare, meat was a luxury, and the water did not run. "Just those, like, those small little things I kind of take for granted here. I look around, and I'm just like, 'Here are roads, and we have cars, and we're living in a home, we're clothed, we're sheltered, we have all of this food.' And it's just things they didn't have access to," he said.' Those small little things compelled his parents to make "their decision to coming over, and making this life so, so exponentially better for us, and them, as well."

His parents' lives before they came to Alabama didn't feel like they had much to do with Brandon's life in Clanton, a groggy town just south of Birmingham. "They heard of this opportunity to escape this lifestyle," as Brandon put it, and if he had been in their shoes, hearing about a chance to go to a place that could offer something better, he would have taken it, too. "You have to find it, you have to seek it; it's not going to be handed to you," he told me. "They went through hell and high water to come over."

They were seeking something better than they had. Mexican migrants in the 1990s "came of age during and after the decline of Mexico's economic and rhetorical support for social justice and the poor," Julie M. Weise writes in *Corazón de Dixie: Mexicanos in the U.S. South Since 1910*. Brandon's parents are from the state of Veracruz, on the eastern coast, a place of tropical cities, beaches, and jungles I have spent time in as a journalist. It made sense to Brandon that they had given up everyone and everything they knew to land in Alabama. To go all the way to the

United States, have to return to Mexico, and then come back with a fifteen-month-old baby. But it was almost coincidental that his family had ended up here; one thing led to another. After working in other states, Brandon's dad, Gilberto, found steady work at a company based in Selma, and the town of Plantersville was close. "It was practical," Brandon said. And his mom hated the cold.

His first memories were of Alabama, they had nothing to do with Mexico. He remembered being little in Plantersville, a one–Main Street town in central Dallas County that was named for the planters and plantations once in it. Before the Battle of Selma, Union troops had stopped in Plantersville to burn the railroad depot and a cotton warehouse. Brandon, his older brother, and his parents lived in a small home "right in front of the train tracks," he said. A patch of woods and a creek ran behind their house, and the bent-over trees had what local people called the "old man's beard." His mom worked most of the day at a plant nursery, and his dad had jobs in construction; Brandon had a babysitter named Vicky. Even then, he remembered that his mom, usually wearing a long-sleeved shirt tucked into jeans, looked tired. He was friends with the boy who lived next door, who came over to play with the packing peanuts that came in their packages and to drink root beers on Brandon's porch. "I guess like the American Dream, right?" Brandon asked me. "They had a home, had a family, had a job to go to." I agreed; it did seem like a version of the American Dream that had lured his parents to Alabama—and, in a more roundabout way, mine, too, long after they thought they would return to Nigeria.

Brandon's is the modern Alabamian family. Except they could be deported at any time. The whole family is undocumented. The Immigration Reform and Control Act of 1986 gave a level of freedom to almost three million people who became newly legalized. It provided amnesty to undocumented immigrants who arrived in the country before 1982. But Brandon's parents were too late for that, though they came to Alabama as a result of the chain migration that pulls in new immigrants' families and friends to a place and spurs the opening of shops and restaurants catering to their community. After meeting Brandon, I wanted to protect him. He is so earnest, he reminds me of a little boy playing grown-up. He is on the shorter side, with low-cut dark hair and the most gentlemanly southern accent I have ever heard, all "yes, ma'ams" and "no, ma'ams."

Even if the state doesn't recognize it, or chooses to only sometimes, it is his home. "As far as I can remember, Alabama has been my home probably since, I dare say, since I was like three or four," Brandon said. "So very, very long back." (Sixteen or seventeen years is a very, very long time for a twenty-year-old.) Brandon is so committed to being part of this place that he has never met most of his relatives, except for one of his grandmothers, who visited from Mexico on a tourist visa for a few months. The rest he sees through screens, instead of touching and holding them. It is tough, he said. "I don't have that opportunity to go back and come again. And I don't know if I'll ever get a chance to. That's the scary part about it."

After Plantersville, his parents moved the family to Maplesville, another tiny town about a fifteen-minute drive north, where they lived on a dirt road in front of a pond filled with bullfrogs; the sounds of them at night terrified Brandon. The family later moved to a single-wide trailer that Brandon's dad converted into a double-wide, closer to Clanton, which had a no-alcohol-sales rule on Sundays until 2021.

Brandon worked for much of his young life picking fruits and vegetables out in hot fields in the summer. His first job was picking blueberries at five years old, following his mom to the field; she couldn't afford a babysitter, so she taught him what to do. Some people would call it traumatizing, being out in the field so young, Brandon knew, but he has chosen to appreciate the experience. It taught him the value of hard, even if it felt thankless, work. They were not that stereotype, he wanted to say, not lazy Mexicans who didn't want to work and fed off the government. He resented that idea; every Mexican he knew worked their ass off.

Summer after summer, Brandon picked in the fields, not thinking much of it. That was his life; it was what he knew. And his mother was smart: she managed to work for people who treated them decently. Then, when he was thirteen, Alabama passed the Beason-Hammon Alabama Taxpayer and Citizen Protection Act, or H.B. 56. An "anti–illegal immigration" bill, H.B. 56 was modeled after a similar one in Arizona that targeted undocumented Latino migrants and was designed to make them leave the state. The bill caught on in Alabama because the growth of the Latino population—which was still only 3 percent of the state at the time—had both revived fading towns and allowed politicians to whip up xenophobia. The bill gave police power to demand papers proving citizenship or legal status whenever they made routine traffic stops. It also required school officials to find out whether students were undocumented; forbade residents from giving rides to undocumented people; stopped employers from hiring people whom they suspected of being undocumented; and prohibited undocumented people from applying for jobs. Latino residents received notices that their water service would be cut if they did not prove their legal status, and some men were too afraid to take their wives to the hospital to give birth. Brandon's mom must have felt that aspect deeply. By making life so untenable for the undocumented in Alabama, the bill's supporters hoped that many of the newer arrivals to the state would "self-deport," as politicians put it. Alabama's first Black federal judge, U. W. Clemon, said at the time that "the Hispanic man is the new Negro . . . It's a sad thing to say."

After the bill passed, thousands of kids didn't show up to school in Alabama. Between the start of the school year in 2011 and February 2012, 13.4 percent of Latino students withdrew from public schools. Brandon was one of a few Latino students at his school, and his friends asked him if he had a green card, if he could bring it to school—and they asked this in front of his teachers. His classmates understood the fear those questions would provoke in him, but not the repercussions they could bring. Brandon felt like the world revolved around his not having legal status, and it was scary. There were days he didn't go to school, just to avoid the questions. H.B. 56 and the arrival of his teenage years were when he realized that not having a Social Security number so he could apply to advanced academic programs or not being eligible to get a driver's license were the kind of disadvantages that would determine his life, placing limits on it before Brandon even had a chance to begin.

Much of what stuck out from that time was the feeling that the people he looked to for guidance were helpless. "Mom and Dad didn't know what to do, their friends didn't know what to do, a lot of people packed up and left, a lot of people went to other states, a lot of people sold what little they had and returned to their country," he remembered. "Racial profiling was a thing. They were pulling people over, and finding reasons and motives why to detain them and then send them off to jail, and then start processing them and start deporting them. It was crazy how rapid things were happening." But his family decided to stay. One day at a civil rights memorial, Brandon connected with the Alabama Coalition for Immigrant Justice, a grassroots organization that advocates for immigrant rights.

I had also gotten in touch with the organization, wanting to talk to them about their work against H.B. 56. The group was made up mostly of immigrants who had jobs and school and families and a lot to lose, but who also felt compelled to stand up for themselves and their neighbors. People who refused to leave their home. They suggested I talk to Brandon. When we met in a park in Clanton, I immediately saw why: he was exceedingly well spoken, gracious, and charming. He seemed far more mature than twenty, but became giddy like a kid when he told me he had gotten a new job.

Because he spoke both Spanish and English fluently,

Brandon was asked to be one of the faces of the sudden movement against H.B. 56, talking to the media and the public to explain how his community was being affected. He marched and participated in vigils, and he spoke and spoke. He even went to Washington, D.C., to speak to an Alabama congressperson. While his classmates went to the beach during the summer, he focused on working in the field and preparing speeches for rallies at the state capitol. Protestors wore T-shirts that read, "We Love Alabama. We Are Alabama." But as much as Brandon wanted to protest, there was the high chance that his classmates and teachers could see him on the news and he would have to explain that he was undocumented and "wasn't born here." Another student did see him on TV and asked if it was really him. Brandon denied it; he was scared. "But as I grew up and matured, and was more socially active in marches and rallies, I kind of realized my identity there with those people," he said. "I realized, 'I am an immigrant.' Obviously, I'm Mexican. I have other ethnicities within my blood. I'm not ashamed. I haven't caused any trouble. I'm an immigrant living in the South. Being socially involved like that, I had power. I had the power of telling my story."

Brandon had spent so much time being afraid of who he is, the story of his life, that he didn't understand he belonged in Alabama as much as anyone else. His activism would help him see that no one had more or less of a claim to it than he did. He may not have had ancestors who were its first inhabitants, or who settled it, or who were forced to pick its cotton, or who fought in its wars, but he knew the land as well as anybody, and more than most. He used an evocative metaphor to describe his journey: people walking out of the shadows. It seems apt for the reality that the face of the green in Alabama is no longer a white good ol' boy farmer and never has been, or at least not its only face. In the shadows are the first Black Alabamians who worked the land to stay alive and the brown immigrants who now cultivate its crops to make a life.

At school, Brandon joined lots of academic clubs and the school historical society, and he hosted events like the talent show and beauty pageant; he loved to talk to people. He also watched his friends and classmates start to drive and get cars and pick up after-school jobs. "That's when it struck me: 'I can't get a really awesome job working at, I don't know, something other than being in the heat,'" he recalled. "Can't really get a car because I really don't have a good-paying job, and how do I get a job? And if I get a job, how do I drive? So, everything was all interconnected, and it was just overwhelming." But when he was sixteen, he found out he was eligible to become a Dreamer, a status named after a federal bill that would have allowed young undocumented immigrants to gain U.S. citizenship through going to college, working, or enlisting in the armed services. The DREAM Act was introduced as a bill in 2001 and has never become law. But in 2012, then president Barack Obama set up Deferred Action for Childhood Arrivals, or DACA, enabling children who came to the country before turning sixteen to gain work permits. When Brandon got clearance his senior year, he was excited to apply for a scholarship to go to community college.

He didn't receive it due to complications with his legal status, though, and suspects that a student who had citizenship got it instead. So Brandon decided to start working. His first job was as a sales rep for an established company; he worked in an office with air-conditioning, wasn't exhausted at the end of the day. He felt normal, something he hadn't felt in a long time. He and his mom were both also working as sales reps for Omnilife, a Mexican multilevel marketing company that made dietary supplements. The job required them to sell door-to-door and make presentations and deliveries, and it let Brandon's mom do something besides work in the fields.

In 2013, a federal lawsuit filed by the Southern Poverty Law Center and other civil rights groups resulted in a settlement agreement with Alabama that struck down most of H.B. 56. It was bad for business: construction and landscape companies lacked workers, crops rotted. But when Trump won office, the fear and uncertainty that had thickened the atmosphere when H.B. 56 was alive resurfaced. Trump wanted to get rid of DACA, and Latino Alabamians didn't know if they would be intimidated again into leaving. What Brandon did know was that his family hadn't gone anywhere and did not intend to. They worked hard, were valuable members of society. Brandon had a good-paying job, he had a car, and he was helping sustain the family. When something in the house needed repair or a car needed fixing, he pitched in to cover costs. "It's magnificent," he said of his ability to do so.

One summer during his last years in high school, he picked potatoes with his mother. His mom has a photo of the two of them working on that big farm one really hot day: Brandon has a bucketful of potatoes beside him. When the photo was being taken, he had stepped outside his body and looked at himself. He had not received the benefits of DACA yet, and he wondered if the rest of his life would be like that captured moment. He had studied so much, done well in his classes, but the only thing he could legally do was put his hands into the dirt. "It brought me to my senses," he told me. "It really took away a lot of determination and motivation. Just seeing myself in that current situation, and thinking, 'I can't do anything better than this.'"

The folktale of individual responsibility, the myth that white Alabamians don't often receive some kind of advantage, was still in his way. Brandon had learned from H.B. 56 that nobody could make him leave his home. He was appropriately grateful for the opportunities he had already received, but he still wanted to be, deserved to be, freer and not made to feel like that freedom was the result of "special treatment"—anathema down here. He wanted to be able to get a scholarship to college, buy a home, invest in assets. His ordeals had produced a defensiveness in him, an armor that made him dig his feet into the dirt of his home, but that is still sheer and porous.

He doesn't have hate in his heart, and he moves through life with that openness. "I want you, at some point, to be shocked, right? I want you to be shocked if you see me on the news, if you see me somewhere, and realize the lies and the things that are said about immigrants," he told me. "You never questioned where I came from, you never questioned what my life was like, you never questioned if I was a citizen or not. I was your friend because I was your friend, and you got to know me. People who don't know my situation, I'm not going to tell them. I want them to discover it through my actions, and I want them to be shocked. Because I feel that makes a stronger impression."

His mom still picked crops, though, and as much as Brandon could celebrate being able to leave that job, it was difficult to see her still doing it. It wasn't right. Every day, when she got home, she told Brandon how terrible she felt. All he could do was sit down with her and listen. Brandon was the only child at home; his brother, who is also a DACA recipient, had moved to Birmingham to start working in banks. "I feel like I owe them a lot," Brandon said of his parents. Now that it was the three of them in the house, three people who understood one another better and could talk more freely as Brandon grew older, he realized he wanted to take care of them. "I could go off, and I could invest in myself and try to do something for myself and worry about me," he told me. "Then I start to think, 'My life is all thanks to Mom and Dad. They took care of me.' I'm thinking, 'No, I should stay. Let me work. Let me try to create this scenario in which I would like to become a little bit more secure with our income.'" Brandon wondered about the day when his father's work in construction would make him feel terrible, too. He believed it was his turn to take over his parents' responsibilities, relieve their burdens, lead the family.

When Brandon and I met up in 2019 in the park in Clanton on one of his few days off, he had just renewed his DACA permit and driver's license. He was one of the first ones at the Department of Motor Vehicles office, and was in and out in about twenty-five minutes. It didn't take too long, but he had to bring his Mexican passport and all his Social Security and work authorization papers, which he was always mindful had not been easy to get and could be revoked by the U.S. government at any time. That day, he again felt thankful for how far he had come from his summers in the fields and for getting a chance to see what that life was like.

I had met few people as humble as Brandon. As people walked and jogged on the paths around us, he told me, "I know what it's like to stress out, know what it's like to get really tired, know what it's like to kind of question my life, and say, 'Do I want to be stuck here doing this? What can I do, where I can go? I don't want to be living in this state, not the state of Alabama, but in this *state*'"—his hands in the dirt, something he thought would never end. "I just felt like, little, so small in the world," he said. Those days were receding, though. On his twenty-first birthday, he bought himself a new Nissan Sentra.

On Thanksgiving weekend in 2022, Brandon was changing his life again. He was leaving his job of three and a half years as an administrator at a home building company for a position at a regional bank. Again, his prospects had flipped in a direction he hadn't imagined for himself. "I just let time roll," he said. Until one day at the gym, he went on, "This gentleman approached me and asked me what I did for a living." The man turned out to be the bank's branch manager, and he was looking for candidates who were bilingual and could help serve the Latino community. Brandon hadn't even told the man he was looking for a job, and had even applied to be a teller at the same bank years ago, but had never heard back. The man saw something in him. "I do tend to lead, rather than carrying that difficulty over my shoulder all the time, with displaying this want and this desire of being successful," Brandon said. People saw it. Brandon attended Mass, but his faith was in himself, a certainty that he could do whatever he put his mind to, if only given the chance.

Two months after sending in the application and going for the interview, he got the bank job. Not only that, but he had bought and renovated a house with his parents, adding a half story on top for his own space. "To continue to live here without being smothered, you know what I mean?" he said, laughing. (Mary McDonald knows what he means; her old trailer in front of her parents' house in the Black Belt was there because of her same need for space and duty to her family.) Brandon also bought a used truck for his father, who lost his own in a car accident, and a 2023 Nissan Murano for his mom. After some time, he moved to working on the corporate side of the bank, instead of the consumer one. He had done so much and wanted more. "We are on the precipice of something brand-new," he told me. I believed him.

* * *

I learned how to bullshit early on in high school. I went to public schools all through my education in Alabama, but starting in seventh grade, I started going to something called a magnet school. It is publicly funded, but reserved for students from all backgrounds and neighborhoods who apply to attend specialized programs.

For ninth grade, I attended an arts and science magnet high school downtown named after Booker T. Washington that offered programs ranging from dance to medicine. Toward the end of that academic year, my dad decided to transfer me to another magnet school downtown, one known for its high-achieving students. I sulked the summer before my sophomore year, angry with him because I wanted to stay with the friends I had known since elementary school. But once I started at LAMP, as Loveless Academic Magnet Program High School is known, I realized I had found my neurotic, nerdy, love-to-talk-and-talk people.

While I was at LAMP, I wanted to be a part of everything. I went through different sports with the delusional confidence found in very young children: I tried out for the tennis team after taking only a few lessons; I started gymnastic classes as a lanky teenager already taller than the teacher; I played indoor soccer, which I loved, but only for a season before I got bored. So I turned to clubs. I liked Model United Nations, but didn't make the traveling team. The activity that stuck was speech and debate. The category I competed in most was called extemporaneous speaking. I can no longer remember if it was I who chose that lane, or my coach, but I do recall being at an event watching people do it and thinking that if those chino-wearing boys could make up shit on the spot that sounded halfway smart, so could I.

Extemporaneous speaking was my best category because I could think quickly and under pressure to come up with rationales for arguments given to me during competition, likely because I had experience arguing with my strict parents for the right to do what I wanted. It was thrilling. You had thirty minutes total to pick a question, look at the research provided, outline an argument based on those sources, and practice some of the speech before you had to actually give it. My best performance came during my senior year, from a prompt about 9/11. The prompt asked why some people around the world had celebrated the attack, and I gave an impassioned speech on how the injustices of U.S. foreign policy were felt abroad and on the dangers of American empire, mostly based on my own curious searching around the internet in the prior weeks. I placed in the top three.

The way to win at speech and debate is to begin with sober key facts, the indisputable details of the given question, and then to emphasize, embellish, flourish. Get worked up, act like your argument is the most logical and just conclusion from the prompt, yet it has somehow never been explored in depth by anyone else until now. You are the first to tell it right, the original storyteller. Be firm, and even a little indignant at times in your entitlement, but not obnoxious. This is the same way, I realized when I got to Princeton and every workplace after that, you need to be to get ahead. I had to slip on the deservedness of a white man and make it mine; it wasn't that hard once you spent enough time around them. For my speech on 9/11, I played to the people way out in the hall. Even if the judges thought I was overdoing it, they seemed to appreciate my unwillingness to show any uncertainty or doubt, a prized quality in Alabama's most popular politicians.

I also competed in dramatic interpretation, a skill akin

to acting, but more premeditated and ruthless. We had to select a piece and then perform the text in a way that felt moving and real. The way to win is to select an emotional monologue from a play or political speech, even though the rules say that "while dramatic elements are key aspects of the event, melodramatic, or overly sad selections are not ideal choices for performance." The idea is to pick a piece related to a serious social issue or personal tragedy and then compel the audience with your interpretation of it; take them on a journey where they feel. Maybe not transformed, but at least impressed. There are no props, costumes, sets, or "other luxuries seen in various forms of performance art," as the rules state. Just you alone or with a partner in front of a bunch of other kids and judges in a too-bright classroom. There is a time limit of ten minutes, with a grace period of thirty seconds if you go over.

I lived for the team's travels to other schools in the South to compete. For a weekend, we pooled into a van driven by our wonderfully goofy coach, Mr. Colvin, and then camped out in a budget hotel. We spent our days in empty classrooms, auditoriums, and cafeterias for the tournaments, competing and hanging out and eating vending machine chips and grilled cheese sandwiches someone was making on a hot plate and selling. Those weekends were when I felt freest as a teenager, beyond the watchful eye of my parents and accountable only to our distracted chaperones. I was sleeping on my own, eating on my own, doing what I wanted within the confines of a high school on its days off; when we were not participating in our events, our chaperones, usually young teachers with uncensored mouths, let us wander with our new rivals and friends and love interests. But we took the competition seriously. I remember practicing with my teammate Heather, a redhead with a prickly resting personality, for a duo event in dramatic interpretation. Our piece was about someone who was heartbroken, or someone who was dying, or maybe someone who was heartbroken and dying. I performed it like I was aging out of the circuit and it was my last competition on earth, which I think was true. After we finished, she turned to me with surprise and said, "That was really good." I was glad she noticed.

Competing was a way of willing myself into belonging, of learning how to argue that reality into being if it didn't happen naturally. Sports had initially seemed like the best way. It's true that Alabamians revere football, but I also watched the confident, sturdy girls who played softball; they had a ready-made set of friends and allies, a place to be every day after school. I was interested in professional sports for a little while, too, memorizing all the American football teams and even collecting baseball cards in a giant binder with laminated sheets. But when my own athletic career stalled, I turned to style and books. I wore delicate blouses and slim skirts from my mom's closet, started accessorizing with my dad's ties, and carried around copies of *The Communist Manifesto* and *The Autobiography of Malcolm X*, books I found revelatory. I fantasized not about escaping my hometown, but about finding my ideal identity within it. I was encouraged to say what I was thinking in and out of class and

I did, a lot, sometimes clashing with my teachers. One math teacher despised me after I argued with him about the 2000 presidential election and then started bringing a big blue Al Gore sign into his class every day. But in Alabama, I learned how to speak my mind and make my way by force, an ability everyone who had stayed shared.

CHAPTER TEN

You Fight

Tina Johnson didn't expect to see Roy Moore's face one winter day in 2017, and she didn't expect to see it on her television with the news that a woman was accusing him of having sexually assaulted her when she was only fourteen. Moore was running for an open Senate seat from Alabama.

"At first I tried to ignore it," Tina recalled. "But residents of Etowah County were getting on CNN, they were getting on national television and saying this girl deserved it, that she shouldn't have been there. That we were marrying people at fourteen back then. They were like, 'Oh, she's lying.' Then they started trying to put Roy Moore and her up to Virgin Mary and Jesus Christ! Saying that Mary was a teenager when she got impregnated with Jesus. And I'm thinking, 'These people are literally ignorant.' So, I said, 'I cannot *not* tell what he done to me. I've got to tell this.' But I didn't realize at that time." She was speaking fast, breathless almost. "I just wanted some-one to know that she wasn't lying. That's all I wanted from it. I just wanted to tell them he done this to me back in his office, and I would believe these girls." It might not have seemed like a lot to some, what Moore did to Tina, but for a past victim of sexual violence, she said, "it brings all that weight and that torture you went through right back, all raw."

Tina had seen Moore on her TV before, when he was still a judge and in the news fighting to have his Ten Commandments monument illegally displayed in the courthouse where he worked. Tina couldn't believe the spectacle he was making: "I had already mentioned to my husband the deal with Roy Moore and my mom and all that, but all I ever said, before that day, was that it was inappropriate. But then, you know, that day, I told him what he done—in 2010. I told my husband what he done." Tina vividly remembered telling her husband, Morris, about Moore grabbing her, because Morris had told her about his own experience going to school in the tiny town of Oneonta. He was one of the only Black kids there, and he cried when he told Tina about the humiliations he experienced at the hands of other stu-dents, like caving in to pressure to grab the behind of a white female classmate. His mother beat him for it, and Morris never got over the shame. Tina had to comfort him. "There was a lot of stuff I didn't know about Roy Moore until this all came out," Tina told me. Not only had Moore been married when he groped Tina that day in his law office, but he had a little girl himself.

Tina decided to email the reporter at AL.com who had written about the recent accusations. She waited a week as the journalist found the court papers proving that Tina had been in Moore's office with her mother. All Tina's silences, big and little, had built up to this point. Her speaking up would mean sticking up for a woman who was being called a liar when Tina knew something of her truth. When Leigh Corfman came out with her story about being sexually assaulted by Moore as a girl, Tina felt it in her body. She had kept her mouth shut about the abuse she had suffered when she was a girl, kept it shut about the indignities afterward. Her mother wouldn't have wanted to listen to her back at the courthouse, when she was excited about Moore's interest in Tina. But now there was someone who cared about what had happened. She could either speak, or watch Moore get away with it again.

"Once AL.com posted, it just went wild," Tina recalled. The press was relentless; they staked out her lawn. At first, her family was resistant to her talking about the assault in public, before coming around, and a few strangers sent ugly messages, but things could have been worse. Tina agreed to be interviewed on TV. She went to New York to appear on Megyn Kelly's show, but she refused to do *The View*. ("It wasn't a good platform 'cause they like to argue too much," she said. I agreed.) She also connected with the other women who had been brave enough to come out against Moore, and they became friends. When the election came around,

Moore easily won Tina's county but lost the state—she had been shocked, and so had I—and things seemed to settle. Some kind of justice had prevailed.

But then Tina's house burned. In the first month of 2018, someone, Tina believed, set it on fire. The night before the fire, she got up three times to turn on the floodlights to see if someone was out on the lawn; her neighbor's dog was going crazy. "There was something out there," she said. The next morning, Tina was not supposed to report for her job at a convenience store, but she went in at the last minute. At about nine or ten a.m., she got a phone call saying her home was aflame. The police detained a suspect caught near the house. It was the same day Moore's Democratic opponent, Doug Jones, was being sworn into office.

Afterward, Tina and Morris moved into a motel room arranged by the insurance adjuster. No one wanted to rent to them once they found out who Tina was, but they finally found a place owned by a man who said he couldn't stand Moore. They were still paying down the mortgage on the burned house, were over twenty thousand dollars in credit card debt, and had rented the new house mostly with donations. They had to buy a bed, clothes, forks. "I was numb. For weeks I didn't eat," Tina said. "When I did eat, it would hurt. It was just horrible." She was upset with the county sheriff's office, which said on the day of the fire, after not having completed an investigation, that it had nothing to do with Moore. In March, the fire department decided that the cause of the fire was inconclusive and that it couldn't rule out a space heater in the laundry room or arson due to ignitable liquids found in the debris. Tina and Morris's insurance company reportedly refused to pay out their full claim. Nothing ever came of the suspect the police interviewed.

"I think I'm being punished," Tina told me. "And . . ." She hesitated, looking at me. "I'm gonna do it. I'm gonna play the race card. My husband is *Black*, and I think they turn it on more on me than they do on him: 'We don't blame you for being with a white woman, but we blame you for being with a Black man.' The insurance adjuster is from Sand Mountain, and there's not even a Black person on Sand Mountain!"

When I visited Tina at her home in Gadsden in the early summer of 2019, she seemed anxious. "Baby," she would begin a sentence. "You just don't know," she would end it. We sat on the couch in her impersonally handsome living room, which looked like it was being staged for the right buyer. "I'm fine," she said, sighing. She wasn't fine. Moore was running for the Senate seat again, in a move that was seen mostly as ridiculous but is now—in light of Trump's continued rallies after losing his own election the following year—kind of normal. If you lose an election fairly, claim it's stolen and run again. If you lose an election because your sexual abuse and harassment are exposed, claim it's a liberal conspiracy and run again.

Tina had just gotten back to Gadsen: the attention from the media and from people in town had been too much. Strangers wouldn't say a lot; they would just "look at me hard," Tina said. They were tired of it, she said, they just wanted it all to go away. So did she. I told Tina that Moore's winning was a long shot. Even conservatives agreed. Voters had other options this time around, like a former Auburn University football coach. But Tina wasn't convinced. "You don't know these crazy folks. Listen, baby, let me tell you something. In my opinion—I don't claim to know anything about no politics, because I don't, but these people are really Bible beaters. I'm not saying there's nothing wrong with that. I'm just saying, though, they'll go with somebody throwing that 'Lord this, Jesus that' crap and fall for it. That's what worries me. They'll go out specifically thinking they're stopping something." Even Tina's husband liked some of what Trump had done. Tina thought he was unfit, a terrible president.

But she still thought of Etowah County as home. She did leave Alabama a few times, like once to move to south Florida for a few years. At the time, her girls weren't older than toddlers. They lived just outside of Orlando. But it was just a blip, and they returned to Alabama. She had even moved to Puerto Rico, working to inventory Walmarts over there. "I always came back here," Tina said. But she had never voted in a single election; she never felt it would make a difference. She was beginning to feel differently now, though. Some things did matter, like supporting good people. Months down the line, the former football coach would win, but she knew Moore still had his devotees. "I've already been medicated and everything—I had real bad anxiety, nightmares, and always looking over my shoulders; it's just too much," she said.

Recently, Tina was getting her car serviced at the Toyota place in town when she overheard a group of people in the waiting room, including an elderly couple, talking about the MeToo movement. They said the women accusing Moore were lying. "And I'm sitting right there! And they don't even know who I am," Tina said. "They were saying that it was too coincidental. And I'm just sitting there listening to it. I was like, 'Oh Lord Jesus, have mercy.'" She didn't say a word. She just got up and walked out.

When Tina was out in town, she never knew what could happen. Once, she was with one of her daughters at Johnson's Giant Food, getting groceries, when a woman recognized her and came up to them. Tina's daughter was sure the woman was going to say something rude, and was getting ready to shoot her down, when the woman thanked Tina. She told her she believed her and thought she was brave for coming out. Tina thanked her, too. But they still hadn't been back to church regularly yet. Tina had gone a few times, but Morris wouldn't go. She didn't know if he was embarrassed, and he wouldn't talk to her about it when she asked him. He was tired on the weekends, she reasoned, from helping out his parents, who lived nearby. And she couldn't blame him. "I miss it, but it wasn't the same," Tina said of church. "People didn't hug me that hugged me before. It's like a wall's built up. It ain't my imagination neither." Normally, when she went up to the altar at church to pray, the elders came up to join and put their hands on her. They no longer did. Even the minister and his wife seemed cold.

It wasn't that Tina was a super-religious person who needed to be at church all the time, but going every week had given her comfort, a sense of belonging. To have that taken away seemed unfair, and so she tried to reason it out, too. "You know, I didn't go for them, anyway. But you still got to worship with people that are right. You can't go with a bunch of devils," she said. "I look at it like, this is what it is, and the Lord meant for me not to be there. That's the way I look at it. But it's not going to change anything. I'm not going to not live right because of them. I'm not going to hurt anybody or anything like that."

It was a trying time. In the spring of 2018, Moore had filed a lawsuit alleging a "conspiracy" and defamation. The defendants were four of his accusers, including Tina. With both the suit pending and Moore announcing his intention to run again, people were calling the house at all hours wanting interviews, asking for comments. "We just took off," Tina said. She and two of her grandkids went down to her sister's place in Florida, and then to Gulf Shores, where they spent much of their time by the beach. Nobody paid attention to them. Morris didn't like that Tina fled, but he didn't argue. She was watching the lawsuit but staying out of it as much as she could, apart from the emotional support she offered to the other women.

As of fall 2024, Moore's defamation case against Tina was still undecided. She was nervous about what else could happen: "I don't know what's coming," she said. In all honesty, she felt abandoned by the MeToo movement. "The women that come out—once you come out, it's all great, but then it's like, who cares? 'I still need you! I need the support. Don't leave me now,'" she said, bubbling over, knowing she was on to something real, a flaw in all the activism.

When the MeToo movement got underway in late

2017, things seemed like they could have turned out differently. It was a surreal moment, when the sexual trauma many women held took on a currency more potent than most of us had thought possible. People were listening, they said; they were believing; they were trusting. Women could suddenly take back their power if they just told their truths about what they had experienced. Storytelling was how to get that currency, taking over the narrative, controlling it. Many of us started thinking back, replaying past sexual experiences in our heads, getting lost in the gray and angry about the obvious. Tina was taken by surprise. Growing up, she hadn't heard any of this talk about believing women. So, when she decided to call that reporter, it was in the feeling of that opening.

We all knew that MeToo would be a little more contested down south, unlikely to catch on quickly in a place with more patriarchal pieties. Tina knew what her people were like. Yet in those first weeks of November 2017, until Moore lost the election the next month, really, and her house burned down at the start of 2018, it seemed worth it. People donated almost two hundred thousand dollars to the GoFundMe that a female tech executive in San Francisco started for Tina and her family after the fire; Tina went to visit her. But when she returned home, her neighbors seemed to be increasingly suspicious about her motives and troubles, and the whole state, even its liberal part, seemed to be fed up with the scandal and the people in it. After the sexual assault news cycle was over, Tina was alone. Nobody seemed to care what happened to her.

The backlash happened around the country. In New

York, I also came to think it was more interesting to ask why people should believe women above all else and not give men some kind of due process—especially because the women we most wanted to believe, the worthiest and most visible victims, seemed to be white middle-class and wealthy women. Black women, other women of color, trans women, and gender nonconforming femmes have to work harder to be given the grace of credibility, never mind poor and working-class women.

Tina is one of those white women whom people wanted to believe and trust. It still wasn't enough. Like she said, if she had to do it all over again, she wouldn't. She's seen how fast those with power can retake control of the story. I asked her if she ever thought of leaving Alabama, getting away from her past, and from the present, too. She didn't stop to think. "My mother instilled in us that you can push me home, but that's as far as you can push me," she said. "You fight."

* * *

Early in 2020, about nine months before the presidential contest that would either reelect Donald Trump or elevate Joseph Biden to office, I was on a tiny plane bumping its way through the clouds from Atlanta to Montgomery. I was traveling from New York to do some reporting and to see family. It was dusk, the sky a deep violet darkening the oval windows, and I was sitting in the front row, my earphones in as I read a book. A single flight attendant greeted passengers with a smile and, as usual, told us the forty-or-so-minute flight was too short for her to serve refreshments, but to let her know if we needed anything.

To the left of me was a woman, white and blond and middle-aged, clearly restless and bored. She kept fidgeting, putting her feet up on the barrier in front of us, then curling her legs underneath her and stealing looks my way with a grin. After we started taxiing down the runway, it didn't take long for her to turn and ask me what I was doing in Alabama. I took out my earphones, and we talked about our respective hometowns—hers was a small town I had been to often as a kid while visiting family friends. And then we somehow got to the topic of the election.

We waltzed around our political affiliations. I assumed she was conservative, but held on to the possibility that she was not, and thought that she probably assumed I was liberal. Normally, according to convention, that difference meant we would avoid talking about politics, steer our talk instead toward family and church. The last thing either of us wanted was to be impolite.

Not this time. She was most worried, she began to tell me, about "ballot harvesting," a term Republicans often used for what they called the manipulation of absentee ballots: the supposed practice of Democratic-leaning middlemen faking signatures on the ballots of unsuspecting voters to steal races. Look it up, she said, it was a big deal. I said I would. I had never heard of ballot harvesting, and when I did look it up on my phone a little while later, most of the reports I read called the threat of it overblown, a scare tactic to limit the use of absentee and mail-in ballots. We were months before a presidential election where absentee ballots would be a crucial determining factor, more essential than ever during a pandemic, a racial uprising, and an economic depression, but back then, her worries about them seemed weird and obsessive. They turned out to have been prescient. Supporters of ballot collecting say that, when done right, it helps expand voting access to groups who are traditionally left out of the democratic process: disabled, poor, and older people; residents of Indian reservations.

Not seven years earlier, the Supreme Court had struck down parts of the 1965 Voting Rights Act in response to a legal challenge from Shelby County in central Alabama. According to the Court's ruling, the state will no longer have to get federal approval to change its election laws, because the discriminatory practices that had demanded the act's passage in the first place—the eligibility tests, special qualifications for poor and Black people, and intimidation of Black voters—were thought not to be a problem anymore. Never mind the restrictive policies and laws that the state has tried to pass since. Twenty-four hours after the Supreme Court decision, Alabama approved a photo identification law that it had tried to put in place in 2011, but had been unable to because the Voting Rights Act had deemed it an unnecessary burden on minorities. Voters will now need an active photo ID, even though Black and Latino voters are usually the least likely to have one. In 2015, the year after the photo ID law took effect, Alabama announced plans to close thirty-one part-time driver's license offices, many of them in Black communities. Driver's licenses are the most common form of ID. The reason for the closures, the state said, was budget cuts. After a federal investigation, the state agreed to expand hours at several offices instead.

Alabama didn't give up. The state added a new requirement to vote in federal elections: proof of citizenship. In 2016, a federal judge blocked the change. By November 2016, we had at least sixty-six fewer polling places than we had in 2013, the time of the *Shelby County v. Holder* decision. Throughout the state, polling stations were closed in districts with meaningful numbers of Black residents. In Daphne, a town of 26,000 outside Mobile, three such stations were closed in 2016.

Our conversation on the plane went on. I had given up on both reading and listening to music. Each time my seatmate brought up ballot harvesting—she kept finding a way—or warned me about voter fraud, she would end her last sentence with a burst of awkward laughter as she searched my face for reassurance. It had happened in Alabama, too, she said, when we were flooded with out-of-state funds and volunteers to help Doug Jones, the Democratic Birmingham lawyer, defeat Roy Moore during the Senate race in 2017. Yeah, Moore was an accused pedophile, but weren't outside agitators worse? And then a wild grin. As if she knew what she was telling me was possibly offensive, but was determined that I hear it for my own good.

Months later, amid a roiling second wave of coronavirus infections around the country, early voters around Alabama would have to wait in long lines at polling stations to cast their ballots; many of those voters, judging from news photos, were Black. Voter suppression has always been part of our narrative. But so has the act of showing up anyway.

Amendments

It depends on who is doing the looking, and it matters where they start the story. For much of this particular story, I've told it as a supporting character who originally wasn't given many lines. I've cast most of the people I've written about here in the same position, on the fringe, trying to break through and get a word in where it counts. But that's not exactly fair. As much as Alabama's storytellers have left things out of their history, so have I—and will continue to do so. It's only my right. But there are parts I want to include, if only for the sake of transparency and to acknowledge that uneasy truth: whoever is telling a story has the power to distort it, will usually distort it for their own ends. But at least we can admit it.

Alabama has the worst prisons in the country when it comes to murder in custody (eight times the national average); suicide (mostly in solitary confinement);

assaults by officers, including excessive force and rape; and drug trafficking by staff. Sexual assaults happen in "dormitories, cells, recreation areas, the infirmary, bathrooms, and showers at all hours of the day and night," a U.S. Department of Justice report said. The prisons are the most violent in this nation. They are also severely overcrowded; some 90 percent of inmates eligible to receive parole are denied it. In 2023, the Alabama Parole Board denied release to an eighty-year-old man with good behavior who had served more than half his life in prison. Activists have a plea regarding the system: prison sentences shouldn't be death sentences. So many times, they and relatives of prisoners who have been murdered, or who have committed suicide, or who have overdosed on drugs, have gathered with photos and stories to march, demanding that state politicians take the crisis seriously. But instead of spending money on mental health and drug rehabilitation programs, the state focuses on the for-profit prison industry. In 2022, Alabama hired a private contractor to build the most expensive prison in American history at a cost of one billion dollars. Elmore County would host a four-thousand-bed correctional facility for an amount of money that is basically equal to the entire budget of the Alabama Department of Mental Health; the state leadership's priorities are clear.

The firm that received the contract to build the men's prison, Caddell Construction Company, is based in Montgomery and has had billions of dollars of work building prisons around the country. One of its executives told a journalist, "I wouldn't want to live in the correctional facilities that we build." The U.S. Justice Department filed a federal lawsuit against the State of Alabama and its Department of Corrections over its belief that the state "fails to provide adequate protection from prisoner-on-prisoner violence and prisoner-on-prisoner sexual abuse, fails to provide safe and sanitary conditions, and subjects prisoners to excessive force at the hands of prison staff." After the Department of Justice released a report detailing widespread abuses in 2019, Governor Ivey promised to do something, saying in a statement that the problem of Alabama's prisons had supposedly "been kicked down the road for the last time." The suit is going forward.

My people are Africans who came to Alabama, but they are also people who became Alabamians. My parents grew used to the way of life, so much so that when they visited me in New York while I was living there, the housing density, noise, trash, and lack of space to breathe repulsed them. My mom's Nigerian accent has faded, and my dad has become obsessed with Alabama college football. My brothers—one of whom went to Auburn and also got obsessed with his team—and I thought of ourselves as American first, with no constraints on what we could do with that identity. But like Black Alabamians who make up just over a quarter of the state but who also constitute more than half its prison population, we were affected by that racist legacy and lost someone we loved in those prisons.

For decades, patrols protected what was once the country's most valuable commodity: enslaved people. The policed status of Black Americans is as old as the nation, stretching from slavery to the Black Codes, which controlled the movement and behavior of formerly enslaved people; on to segregation and the growth of prisons, which currently take in African Americans at five times the rate of white people nationwide. The effect has been the surveillance and punishment of Black Americans for the comfort of their white neighbors, and of poor Americans for the security of wealthier ones. At the end of 2023, a group of Black former and current prisoners, with others, sued the state of Alabama for practicing what they called a "modern-day form of slavery" by forcing the incarcerated to work menial jobs with little or no pay for private companies and government agencies, while disproportionately denying parole to Black prisoners, including ones eligible for those jobs.

The details of our loved one's death are not important to these amendments—or maybe they are and I just don't want to tell them—but I include the fact to make the story a little more complete. We achieved a version of the southern American dream and were heartbroken by it, too. We gained the best of what it has to offer to new arrivals and their offspring and experienced it in the deadliest way possible. Americans are comfortable living with inherent contradictions, and Alabamians are no different.

People not from Alabama like to assume my upbringing was defined by my race, more so than an upbringing in any other state could be. But the truth is that, despite experiencing racism at times, I was not scarred in any memorable way, a privilege I can ascribe to being middle class and going to racially mixed schools. The moment I became aware of being a Black person was memorable, though. Frantz Fanon wrote about the moment of being a young boy in France with his mother when he heard a white child say, "Maman, regarde le nègre, j'ai peur!" ("Mom, look at the Black person, I'm scared!") I, on the other hand, was a young child in a McDonald's in Montgomery with a few dollars my dad had given me to buy french fries. I got in line behind a group of white teenage girls, probably in high school and intimidating in my eyes. They were talking with an employee, and one girl turned around to look at me and then told the others that it was "just a little Black girl" waiting behind them. The comment hit me almost like an insult, even though it was not likely one. I felt exposed, and aware that this new knowledge of how others saw me would change my life from then on. I stayed in line and got my fries, though.

Brittany Howard, the former lead singer of my favorite band from Alabama, told an interviewer in 2023, "Being [in the South] is so conflicting, because it's in my blood," she says. "And my ancestors have been around since before it was incorporated. Who's to say that this isn't my home just because of my color, or my background, or my sexuality? This is mine, just as much as it is the good ol' boys'. So how do we work it out together?"

We keep trying. The story goes that the Black male politicians of Reconstruction-era Alabama who rose to unlikely power before they fell just as quickly were reviled and chased out by their white neighbors, which is true, but it's more complicated than that. Benjamin Sterling Turner was born enslaved in 1825 in North Carolina, but he ended up in Alabama, stolen from his family. As a young man, he began working in various businesses while still enslaved, could keep some of his earnings, and became financially independent by the time the Civil War broke out. Turner would come to own three hundred acres in Dallas County and have assets worth ten thousand dollars. In his city of Selma, where he helped found a school for Black children, he was appointed county tax collector with support from Black and white voters. After a year doing that, he won a seat on the city council. Later, he became the first Black person from Alabama elected to the House of Representatives. But Turner had a contradictory life, and he wanted seemingly contradictory things, probably the foremost sign that he had become a son of Alabama. He campaigned for Congress on a platform of both universal suffrage and "universal amnesty," which would forgive secessionists in his state and let them hold office again; local carpetbaggers (members of his party born north of the Mason-Dixon line) refused to support him because of it. But Turner had seen the humiliations in bondage and the possible prosperity in freedom, even a freedom that was restricted by those secessionists, and his appreciation of the latter appealed to his white neighbors. "I was pleased enough at the taking of the town," Turner said of the Union military victory in Selma, "and rejoiced until they took everything I had and I got mad." In the 1980s, two Black organizations decided to raise money to put up a monument commemorating Turner in Selma. Fund-raising was initially slow going.

But once the city's white residents were told how instrumental Turner had been in gaining amnesty for their ancestors, the organizers quickly got the money they needed.

* * *

When I was growing up, my hometown's public high schools were racially divided. In central Montgomery,

Jefferson Davis High School was named after the former president of the Confederacy, and Sidney Lanier High School after a Confederate private; both schools were mostly Black. In the 1990s, despite also being midtown (it was zoned for students who lived on the north side), Robert E. Lee High School was mostly white. And so it never caused much of a stir that not only was the school named after a Confederate general, but also standing in front of it was a bronze statue of the man himself. Robert E. Lee opened as an all-white school one year after *Brown v. Board of Education*. At its start, in 1955, the campus cost over $1 million, had $125,000 worth of equipment, and could serve almost eight hundred students. Its marching band wore Confederate uniforms. The *Advertiser* celebrated the opening, writing that it had been "about 26 years since Montgomery had a new white school."

Many white Alabamians had fought under Lee, but the city's moving his statue from downtown to the campus meant more than a tribute to ordinary soldiers. Between 1950 and 1975, as the civil rights movement took off, at least 150 Confederate monuments and memorials were dedicated throughout the South in defiance. When Black activists tried to order lunch at segregated counters or attend white schools, white protestors held up Confederate flags; they hung those same flags along the route of the voting rights marches from Selma to Montgomery. Alabama school boards could get around *Brown* through a state law that allowed for a process called "pupil placement," which claimed to assign students to schools on the basis of ability, academic background, and availability of transportation, but did so according to their race.

These were things I didn't know as a kid. I knew only that Jeff Davis and Lanier had the Black kids and Lee the white ones. But by 2009, Lee had a mostly Black student body. By 2020, three Lee graduates would start a campaign to rename the school, as well as Jeff Davis and Lanier—the least, they felt, the city could do. During the most significant racial uprising the country had ever seen, a petition to rename the schools got the signatures of nearly thirty thousand people. In July of that year, the Montgomery Board of Education voted to rename the school, along with Jeff Davis and Lanier.

The previous month, on the birthday of Jefferson Davis, a state holiday, four people were arrested and later charged with first-degree criminal mischief, a felony, after they toppled the statue of Lee from its pedestal. As protests against the police killing of George Floyd flooded downtown, a crowd assembled in front of the statue, assessing it again. Thinking. Twenty-four hours earlier, another crowd had tried to take down a five-story Confederate obelisk in downtown Birmingham. "Montgomery is full of slave trophies," one protestor in the capital said. After the Lee statue fell, the crowd was heard cheering and singing. Cars surrounded the group and honked their horns. The day after the fall, Montgomery's public school district announced that it had moved the statue to storage, but Calvin Chappelle, as director of the Confederate Memorial Park, heard that the monument was eventually given to the local chapter of the Sons of Confederate Veterans, an organization for the male descendants of Confederate soldiers.

Calvin and I were together one morning in the fall of

2021 with the spokeswoman for the Alabama Historical Commission at the commission's office in downtown Montgomery. Calvin's beard was longer and bushier than I had ever seen it before, hitting the puffer vest he was wearing over a button-down shirt. If I didn't already know him, I wouldn't have thought he was the kind of man I would ever get to know.

The Deep South is a land with no shortage of memories, but the Confederate monuments guided us to the ones that were most valued. Early on, the story of the Confederacy had to be romanticized and made vague; the ideas of self-rule and cultural pride replaced the realities of secession and slavery. Innocent enough to be a fairy tale, suitable for reading at bedtime, the myth was of an industrial North wanting to dominate a pastoral South. To twist the story any other way now requires the combined efforts of everyone whose memories were not turned into concrete. Calvin recognized some of this. He told me, "That's where it all began—who's going to control the narrative in 1866? The North wants to tell their story, the South wants to tell their story. African Americans are telling their own story, but their voices are not being heard."

Momentum had been rising. In 2019, my hometown elected its first Black mayor, a handsome and affable man named Steven L. Reed. I was unaware that Montgomery, Alabama's capital city and home to a Black majority, had never had a Black mayoral leader, seeing as it had had so many other kinds of Black leaders—civil rights ones, religious ones, local power broker ones, societal and cultural ones. How was this possible? Reed put it well at the time, saying that the first enslaved Africans were brought to the country in 1619; Montgomery was founded exactly two hundred years later, in 1819; and he was elected as the city's first Black mayor another two hundred years on. Progress had come, but it had dragged its feet the whole way. Still, there Reed was, trim and clean-shaven and vaguely Barack Obama–styled in button-downs and slim pants, giving an interview to CNN on Election Night about the historical significance of his win; taking the stage at his sold-out inauguration gala in a four-star hotel downtown; unveiling a new bronze statue of Rosa Parks near the stop for the bus she once boarded. Reed was Montgomery County's first Black probate judge. His father, Joseph, was a student at Alabama State University who joined a 1960 sit-in at the segregated restaurant in the Montgomery County Courthouse and was put on probation for it. That same year, Joseph met Martin Luther King Jr.; his son, the new mayor, has a framed picture of them sitting together in a Baptist church in the city.

Despite the glowing profiles of Reed in the national press, I didn't think much about him until the following summer, when southerners all over started demanding that the monuments devoted to the Confederacy near their homes be taken down, whether politely or by force; it was their leaders' choice. Throughout the South, a number of Black mayors—including Randall Woodfin, over in Birmingham; LaToya Cantrell in New Orleans; Frank Scott Jr. in Little Rock; and Stephen K. Benjamin in Columbia—had to decide what to do with the clutter of stone memorials and how to please most of their likely voters in the next election. Not only that, but many of the monuments would be coming down anyway, at the hands of their constituents, and so they had to choose sides fast. Reed had the idea in 2020 to rename Jeff Davis Avenue and call it Fred D. Gray Avenue, after the Alabama State graduate, then ninety, who had represented Rosa Parks and other residents in cases challenging segregation. Gray had grown up on the street. Reed held a renaming ceremony in late 2021, which Gray and his wife attended. Afterward, the state attorney general threatened to sue Montgomery for violating the state law protecting Confederate monuments and memorials, unless it paid a $25,000 fine. But the city wasn't an outlier: several Alabama cities chose to take down Confederate monuments and pay the fine.

A few years later, Reed told the city council, "We are working to shift the narrative surrounding Montgomery to celebrate our real heroes and not those that have long stymied Montgomery's progress." A commission he set up to study the city's ties to the Confederacy recommended renaming at least seven streets. There are more than one hundred monuments in the state, on the grounds of the capitol building and in front of schools and in the center of campus of the University of Alabama and at more than a third of county courthouses. Alabama took down the third-highest number of Confederate symbols in the country in 2020, removing twelve.

I was genuinely surprised my hometown was renaming schools and taking down symbols. Calvin told me he had reached out to Black historian Richard Bailey about his writing on the efforts of Black Alabamians to

make a place for themselves in the state after the Civil
War. He wanted to interview Bailey for an exhibit he was
curating on Civil War memories, which would look at the
ways different groups of people in Alabama had experienced the war. Calvin wanted to know about the early
Emancipation Proclamation celebrations in Alabama,
which started as early as January 1, 1866, and how newly
free Black people had marked the news. Bailey told him
that any gatherings had necessarily happened away
from white eyes, with no or very little money, and so
they often took place in the Black church. Lincoln signed
the Emancipation Proclamation on January 1, 1863, but
Montgomery recognized it only on January 1, 1866. The
Emancipation Association of Montgomery, which com-
memorates the signing every New Year's Day, came
out of the Black church, too. It was the only place safe
enough to acknowledge this declaration of freedom, the
hope that it would be possible to move forward on the
continuum from bondage to liberty, if only a few steps.
The commemoration of the Proclamation is the oldest,
continually running emancipation celebration in the
state, though it isn't a state holiday. Alabama has become
known for the holidays it still chooses to recognize (three
are in honor of the Confederacy) and those it continues to
downplay (Martin Luther King Jr. Day is combined into a
joint holiday with Robert E. Lee Day). But other celebrations still go on, as they always have. On the 150th anniversary of Montgomery's recognizing the end of slavery,
the Emancipation Association in Birmingham held a ceremony at Bethel Baptist Church. U. W. Clemon, the Black

judge who lamented that "the Hispanic man is the new Negro," was a speaker and told the audience that as they celebrated, they had to "do so with a full understanding that the dream of equality is yet before us."

For the state bicentennial in 2019, the historical commission put up a park in commemoration at the base of the capitol. My dad and I drove down one day to see it in the sunlit winter chill; we were skeptical but curious. Heavy bronze panels with text and illustrations stood throughout the park, giving an account of meaningful moments from the state's founding until the present. The first panel we read named the Creek as Alabama's first people. The second talked about the "illegal encroachment by whites" on Creek land and ended with words from a Creek chief named Menawa, on the last time he saw his own land before being forced to go to Indian Territory. Two later panels were named "Reconstruction" and "Constitutional Convention of 1901." At the time I viewed them, I didn't remember ever having heard more than a fleeting lecture about Reconstruction's being a difficult period after the war, when Alabama had to get back on its feet. The panel talked about how free Black people who had hoped to "exercise their new rights of citizenship" were met with widespread violence from whites and the Ku Klux Klan during this time, and mentioned that the state government was briefly integrated. The panel on the 1901 constitutional convention admitted that the state constitution had been ratified in a vote that "again relied on election fraud." Not only that, but it said the vote meant that essentially no Black Alabamians could vote again after the convention ended.

My home state loved to be defiant, and I thought the summer of the 2020 uprising would be no different. But some things had changed. Its storytellers had realized that to stay in control, they would have to make some amendments. Alabama is good at that.

CHAPTER ELEVEN

Betrayal of Your Kin

A few years ago, I was at a party in New York where I met a white woman who started telling me about a project she was doing on the Poarch Creek. I was amazed; I selfishly thought I was the only writer in New York interested in them. The woman had a personal connection to the tribe: she had a relative who was Poarch Creek, but she knew other people who were having trouble proving their belonging. The tribe was stingy when it came to its membership roll, the woman told me. It reminded me of another, lesser-known tribe in Alabama called the MOWA band of Choctaw Indians, at the crossroads of Mobile and Washington counties; MOWA stands for the first two letters of each county in which the tribe resides. Though the state recognizes them, the tribe is accused of not being Indian enough. People say they're Black trying to pass as Indian, for status.

The Poarch Creek's insistence on members having pure enough DNA to belong, in a state where genetic racial boundaries don't exist, is a distinctly Alabamian irony. White people in the South have the most African ancestry of white people living anywhere in the country. For decades, the Poarch Creek wavered precariously in the racial hierarchy: they could legally marry white people, but their children could not attend the same schools as white kids. Many white residents considered them to be of ill repute, and darker-skinned Creek were shut out of whites-only spaces. Indians had an uncertain relationship with their Black neighbors; like white people, the Creek did not want their kids attending school with Black children, either. "Creeks worked hard to maintain social and legal boundaries between themselves and Blacks . . . the ancestors of the Poarch Creek occupied a third position in the area around where they lived, somewhere in between the social and political hierarchy between Black and white," Mark Edwin Miller writes in *Claiming Tribal Identity*. Any Creek heritage that Black Alabamians claimed— and many did claim to have at least some Indian in their blood—had not translated to a mutual feeling of kinship. Elsewhere in Indian country, the Creek had chosen to deny the belonging of Black people who can trace their ancestry to them, until a 2023 Creek court decision allowed in descendants of people enslaved by the tribe.

Alabama eventually recognized nine tribes in the state, but the Poarch Creek remain the only one with federal approval. The other eight tribes can be mostly found in the southeastern part of Alabama, near Dothan and its annual National Peanut Festival, or up north, near

Huntsville and its NASA Space Camp. These tribes and the Poarch Creek have vastly different origins but one important thing in common: their forefathers and -mothers avoided being dragged onto the Trail of Tears. The MOWA Choctaw survived the best way they knew how. During the Creek War, a group of the MOWA Choctaw fought alongside Red Stick Creek warriors against federal troops. When they lost, they fled into the swamps of south Alabama. They knew what was coming. Amid hunger and disease, some survived. As Indian removal was happening in the 1830s, many of their brethren followed them into the swamps and pine barrens, taking shelter for years. To make do, women sold firewood on the streets of Mobile, and men hunted to sell game meat and deerskins. "They hid in the forests," MOWA's tribal chief, Lebaron Byrd, once said of his ancestors. "Some of them hid for years at a time, avoiding troops and law enforcement. The ones who survived settled in this part of the state."

Some MOWA Choctaw were able to gain land through the Homestead Act of 1862. Many of them later worked in timber, harvesting pine sap to turn into turpentine, and barely made enough money to live. They worked for a local Choctaw leader named John Everett, as Jacqueline Anderson Matte writes in *They Say the Wind Is Red: The Alabama Choctaw—Lost in Their Own Land*. Their pay was docked because of debts that piled onto themselves at the general store where they shopped for food and goods. Everett, co-owner of the store, and a white businessman who had interests in timber ultimately repossessed the land of several workers who could not afford to pay their

bills and property taxes. Acres of green for unpaid groceries. Gradually, Choctaw families would relocate out
of the forest to logging camps and then squares of green
along back country roads.

As the years passed, the Choctaw community coalesced
around ceremonial gathering places, burial grounds, family compounds, and then churches and schools. And the
tribe fought its own civil rights battles. In 1970, MOWA
Choctaw leaders stopped the local school boards from
closing their Indian schools; they believed the institutions,
however lacking in resources, were important to preserv-
ing their culture. The tribe succeeded in getting a federal
court order that required one Indian school each in Mobile
and Washington Counties to stay open. As for their families, they mixed with Black folks and white, and could be
described as both of those. One MOWA member was listed
in Alabama censuses, variously, as "free person of color,"
"mulatto," "Black," and "white" throughout his life.

At the end of the 1970s, the MOWA Choctaw won
recognition from the Alabama government. They could
finally benefit from public services meant for Indians,
such as medical treatment, housing, education, and the
care of their children and elders. But in 1997, the Bureau
of Indian Affairs denied their federal petition, meaning
they would not receive the right to govern themselves or
the ability to build gambling wealth. The agency decided
that the MOWA Choctaw did not have enough records
detailing a sustained cohesive existence, absent a long-
running tribal leadership, or a central authority, or a
history of relations with the federal government. (They

had been in hiding, after all.) What they did have—oral histories, kinship ties, shared memories of struggle—the federal government deemed insufficient. Their tangled racial origins in Native, European, and African ancestors defied genetic blood testing. Their tribe was not enough of a tribe. The lines that the Five Tribes, along with the U.S. government, had drawn around Indian identity were meant to define the boundaries of what was acceptable Nativeness, and they also helped keep out groups that complicated racial and ethnic categories.

The Bureau of Indian Affairs decided the tribe was a Black-and-white "mulatto" people with little Native ancestry. The Poarch Creek turned against the MOWA Choctaw, too, after the tribe's former leader promised to back the latter's cause, but later did an about-face and said they weren't a tribe. The Cherokee Nation put them on their fraudulent tribes list. The leaders of the federally recognized Mississippi Band of Choctaw, the MOWA Choctaw's supposed kin across Alabama's western border, have been "overtly hostile to its aspirations," Miller writes. A former U.S. senator from Alabama, Richard Shelby, tried to push for federal recognition of the MOWA Choctaw in recent years, but to not much effect.

Lebaron Byrd, their chief, has said his tribe hasn't given up. Some 6,500 of its members, many of whom live in the shadow of the Poarch Creek's casinos and hotels, still make their home in southern Alabama, on a reservation northwest of Mobile. They have a tribal council, which Byrd still led in 2024 and, by the look of it, included a racially diverse group of members. Their racial makeup was almost their undoing, in more ways than one. After the Black scholar Horace Mann Bond visited the tribe in 1931, he observed that the MOWA Choctaw were caught in limbo between white and Black people because of their rejection by the former and their rejection of the latter. But they are Native and Alabamian, too, and they have also managed to stay.

CHAPTER TWELVE

Betrayal of Your Home

Many of the Black people now living in Lowndes County, whether they have Indian in them or not, are descendants of enslaved people who may have worked the plantations that once thrived throughout the Black Belt. Whether they have low-slung houses with big porches and yards like Mary McDonald or double-wide trailers that sit on plots of green, their families have experienced the entire range of Black being, from liberty on the African continent, to captivity in America, to a kind of mediated emancipation that ebbs and flows in Alabama and the rest of our country. Mary has always thought of her family as rooted here partly because of the house and land they own; and even though young people were leaving Lowndes County for more oppor-tunities, to many of them it would always be home. To possess or reside freely on the land their enslaved and sharecropper ancestors worked is still a source of pride. It's a triumphant story: some of the spoils have returned to their rightful toilers. But what happens if the land turns against you? If your home, after all that struggle to stay on it, betrays you?

Hayneville, the county's one–Main Street seat, is not much to look at compared to the lush fields and forests outside it, but it serves its purpose. There are the telephone company and the town hall (which shares a building with the fire department), the middle school and the public library, the post office and the auto parts shop, the bank and the Family Dollar, the ice station and the pharmacy, some gas stations and Southview Worship Center (which during the Covid-19 pandemic advertised a drive-in service on Sundays at nine in the morning)— most of which have giant, cracked asphalt parking lots. People work for the Hyundai suppliers; or in education, health care, and government; or in retail, manufacturing, and construction; and they tend not to mind the easy commute between their workplaces and the grocery store and church.

But Lowndes also has the distinction of being one of the poorest counties in Alabama; its unemployment rate was 4.8 percent as of March 2024, one of the highest in the state. It is one of seven counties without a hospital. Like much of the Deep South, the state has refused to expand its Medicaid program under the Affordable Care Act. When asked if she would consider expanding Medicaid to help her constituents during the pandemic, Governor Ivey responded that it would be "irresponsible" to expand without considering the effect on the state budget—though federal funds would cover most of the cost. Nearly a tenth of people in Alabama are now uninsured, and health centers in poor communities have had to take on the cost of giving care to patients who cannot pay. Seven rural hospitals in Alabama have closed over the last decade, and many of the rest are losing money and cutting back on services and staff. Lowndes County pays $19,000 a month for a single ambulance to take residents to hospital emergency rooms in the cities.

At a Montgomery City Council meeting in the summer of the first year of the pandemic, things turned contentious when its members deliberated over whether to vote for a citywide mask-wearing rule. A pulmonologist at Jackson Hospital named William Saliski told the council that he and his colleagues had nearly 250 patients at the time, half of whom were on ventilators, 90 percent of whom were Black. Residents of Black Belt towns had been checking into Jackson at an unprecedented rate. Another doctor, Nina Nelson-Garrett, described dead bodies being carried out of her hospital every half hour. A resident of Montgomery, William Boyd, told council members he had lost six relatives to Covid-19. "The question on the table is whether Black lives matter," he said. The council still voted the mask policy down. The next day, Montgomery's mayor, Steven L. Reed, issued an executive order mandating the use of masks in public spaces. At the council's next meeting, a month later, it agreed to a mask mandate. Days on, Alabama governor Kay Ivey finally issued a statewide mask order after a 50 percent increase in new cases. Instead of a stay-at home rule, Ivey recommended a "safer-at-home" order, which advised

Alabamians to remain in their houses as much as they could—even though many businesses, factories, restaurants, gyms, entertainment venues, and stores were remaining open. In other words, when I finally went down to Montgomery that July after being under lockdown in New York for the past three or so months, most people looked at me like I was crazy for wearing a mask in public.

Like everywhere else, the death rate of Black people in Alabama due to Covid-19 was more than twice the rate of their white neighbors. Though Black Alabamians make up just over a fourth of the state's population, they were nearly half the people dying. Black residents were getting sicker than anyone else. Lowndes County had the highest per capita death rate and at the peak of its crisis, in June 2020, an infection rate that neared that of New York City at its worst. More than a third of tests were coming back positive. Lowndes residents were working essential jobs and living in close quarters, which put them more at risk—but they were also living amid one of the worst environmental crises in the country, which made the pandemic even deadlier.

They are *still* living amid one of the worst environmental crises in the country. There are no public sewer systems in much of rural America, never mind in the country in Alabama. Most residents of the Black Belt are forced to invest in on-site septic systems or rely on pipes that run waste straight into their yards. The septic systems can cost up to thirty thousand dollars, only a few thousand dollars less than the area's median annual household income. But even that technology often fails. Because it is made up of a thin layer of dirt atop impermeable clay, the region's dense, dark soil that was once good for growing cotton prevents the absorption of waste, sending sewage back into the house through toilets and sinks and bathtubs. Half the private septic systems in Lowndes County have failed or are expected to. The region's high water table, along with more frequent rain due to climate change, contributes to conventional septic tanks and dirt mound filtration systems backing up and falling apart.

And so, sewage is everywhere: in a sickly green lagoon in Hayneville, next to a row of houses; in ponds; on roads; in people's yards and homes. It's what Philip Alston, the United Nations' special rapporteur on extreme poverty and human rights, called, while on a visit to the Black Belt in 2017, some of the worst poverty he had seen in the developed world. "This is not a sight that one normally sees," Alston told AL.com, seeming shaken. "I'd have to say that I haven't seen this."

He probably hadn't seen what Alabama does to people living in those conditions, either. Residents, mostly Black and poor, who don't comply with laws to keep installing and maintaining flawed septic systems are criminalized, subject to fines, arrest, and eviction. A pastor in the little city of Brundidge, which has both a Hardee's and a country club, was arrested in 2014 because his church didn't have a functioning septic tank. For years, activist Catherine Flowers, with the help of residents like Mary McDonald, had been documenting septic failure in people's homes and trying to get the state to adopt new technology. Once they got the help of researchers from

Baylor College of Medicine, they realized something else: because of all the sewage, many Black Belt residents had contracted hookworm and other tropical parasites thought to have been eradicated from the American South. It was a goddamn crisis.

Before the pandemic, Catherine had taken me to meet a sweet, unassuming woman named Pamela Rush, who lived in a pale blue single-wide trailer on a tangerine-dirt road outside the Black Belt town of Troy. Cell phone service is hard to come by there. The late civil rights leader John Lewis grew up poor in the same stretch of countryside. Pamela's home was surrounded by thick woods, and her sister Almedia lived in a trailer in front of her. Pamela had been living in the blue trailer since she was a young woman taking care of her aging mother; the family bought it in the mid-1990s. Pamela parked it in her yard and used a pipe to empty the household waste straight into the grass below—the practice, called straight-piping, is not rare in the Belt or much of rural America. The raw sewage in Pamela's yard contributed to the mold and mildew inside. There was mold in her nine-year-old daughter Bianca's bedroom, where the power didn't work. Because she needed a CPAP machine to breathe while she slept, Bianca spent most nights in the living room. Pamela's son Jeremiah, who was sixteen, also lived with them; he had a learning disability and was still in middle school. Pamela had to stuff rags into gaps in the walls of her trailer and set traps outside the door—she had caught four opossums so far, and other animals. The situation had gotten so bad that Pamela's sister Barbara decided to send a Facebook message to Catherine, asking for help. Another of Pamela's sisters, Viola, had been arrested in the past for a sewage violation.

After bringing a series of high-profile visitors to Pamela's home, including Vermont senator Bernie Sanders, to show them the toll of the emergency, Catherine received a donation to buy a new double-wide trailer for Pamela and her kids. The trailer was energy-efficient and would come with a new septic tank (that might or might not prevail). Pamela was elated. Meanwhile, Catherine was still trying to get the health department to treat the sanitation disaster as a public health matter, rather than one of personal responsibility. She and Mary and other volunteers had done a door-to-door survey of most residents in the community. The prevalence of diabetes— which often went unchecked because people couldn't afford to see a doctor regularly to manage it—high blood pressure, and breathing problems stemming from asthma and smoking weren't increasing the chances of people contracting Covid-19, but they were making it likely the infected would have a bad time of it.

It took a while for the people of Lowndes County to realize the extent to which the virus had spread around them. In the summer of 2020, I went back to Pamela's home. Her sister Barbara had contracted the coronavirus from her factory job, and had recovered; her sister Almedia had also gotten it. In June, Pamela thought she had a sinus infection. She had a cough, lost her appetite, and had trouble with her sight. When she went to see a doctor in Selma, staff checked her vital signs and found that she had pneumonia. She then tested positive for Covid-19, and the clinic sent her on to a hospital in Birmingham. During her first days there, Pamela's family told her not to be afraid, and she promised she wasn't. She even asked for her eyeliner. But over the next week her body began to shut down, and she was put on a ventilator. On the day before the Fourth of July, she died. Her home-going service was held on a hot Saturday at a church in Lowndes County. Dozens of her relatives and friends attended. Her son wept inconsolably.

Pamela's home had betrayed her, but it was still her home. Land here is fickle like that, inviting owners and then expelling them, their blood living on in the soil as the next ones come to take their place.

* * *

To this day, one of my closest friends from Alabama is a girl I met my sophomore year of high school, after I transferred to the academic magnet program. I immediately noticed her because she was exceedingly smart, a trait I valued highly, and unabashed about her smartness, another trait I valued highly. She was a girl who spoke up everywhere: in class, outside class, around Black kids, around white kids, to teachers and other adults. But she also knew how to code-switch between a wry outspoken-ness and an ingratiating politeness; after all, she was a member of Jack and Jill, the Black social organization that held cotillions. Her hair was relaxed dead-straight, and she knew her mind.

Her name is Elizabeth, and we ended up going along parallel paths for a while. She also left Alabama for college—she went to Harvard—and then lived in

New York and Los Angeles. For years after we left high school, through college and our first jobs, we would meet up over drinks or lunch or dinner, and if the topic of our home state came up, the mood would sometimes get a little tense. If it was an election year, I would complain that there was no use for Democrats to even try down here, and she would get defensive. It wasn't right, she would say, to dismiss voters in Alabama and what they felt about social and economic issues and the potential for those attitudes to change with the right kind of persuasion. I would laugh; she couldn't be serious. Alabama was a lost cause. Most everyone in it had made up their minds about how they believed the country should be run, and who should benefit, and those who disagreed, like Elizabeth's and my families, were vastly outnumbered.

But after Roy Moore lost and Doug Jones won the Senate seat, there was something in the air. Not optimism, exactly, but a kind of hopeful buzzing. Jones is the right kind of Alabama Democrat, a beloved prosecutor who finally convicted the KKK members behind the 1963 Birmingham church bombing that killed four little Black girls, more than three decades later. It was the first time in twenty-five years that a Democrat had been elected to the Senate from the state, and some organizers thought it foolish not to see if the progressive energy that had upset what was supposed to have been a sure race could be harnessed into a more long-lasting political presence.

I was curious, too. In the fall of 2018, I got in touch with Hometown Action, which focuses on canvassing and registering voters in rural Alabama. The group said it was nonpartisan; its volunteers called themselves progressive; and I followed them one day in Wetumpka as they canvassed for three female Democratic candidates, including one for Congress. It felt a little novel to be going around with the group of young-leaning people and retirees, having friendly conversations on people's porches about politics and dogs. Their line to me, a good one, was that they were knocking on doors that hadn't been knocked on before, or at least not in a long time—my friend Elizabeth's defense. They knew their home well: they were advocating for social justice issues by appealing to the state's values of family, faith, and hard work. Hometown Action–endorsed candidates had to sign on to the group's goals—racial and gender equity, sustainable communities, fair economies, true democracy, environmental protection, and access to education and health care—things its leader, Justin Vest, called "common sense." But when it came to issues like abortion, Vest was honest with me: "We're still figuring out how to talk about those things."

It hasn't gotten any easier. After *Roe v. Wade* fell in the bleak early summer days of 2022, Alabama began enforcing its abortion ban. Abortion is prohibited at all stages of pregnancy, with no exceptions for rape or incest. Providing an abortion is a felony, punishable by up to ninety-nine years in prison. The state wants to prosecute residents who travel outside Alabama to get the procedure, and the Yellowhammer Fund, which helps people afford abortions, and the West Alabama Women's Center, a former abortion provider—both organizations I have written about—have filed suit, arguing that such prosecution is unconstitutional. (The U.S. Department of

Justice has filed a statement of support in the lawsuit.) The abortion ban is devastating; so is the undercurrent of intolerance. Alabama columnist John C. Archibald called the state a "theocracy" after its Supreme Court defined frozen embryos as children, and the chief justice cited Bible verses in his concurring opinion. The wave of book banning in the country has started to drown public libraries; a county one in Huntsville tried to move seventy children's books with LGBTQ themes to the adult section, until the action was revealed in the local press. The Alabama Public Library Service announced that it would issue a list of books it considers inappropriate for children. A bill that prevents public schools, colleges, and other state agencies from promoting certain "divisive topics" related to race, sex, and religion was signed into law by Governor Ivey in 2024, after another bill, banning talk in the classroom about sexual orientation or gender identity from grades kindergarten through fifth, had passed two years before. Local activists and Democratic state lawmakers are fighting back. In 2024, a Democrat won a special election to the Alabama legislature campaigning against the abortion ban and sharing her own abortion story, and a federal court drew a new, mostly Black congressional district in the state to rectify past disenfranchisement of Black voters. But as it tends to do, progress is dragging its feet the whole way.

CHAPTER THIRTEEN

The First, Part Two

In time, places, for better or worse, can grow on you. You love and hate the places dearest to you. When my parents were students, they probably weren't thinking about the possibility that they would be as much Alabamian as any of their neighbors nearly five decades on. They probably weren't thinking about the possibility, either, of having a child who would use the details of their lives, the big and small choices, to tell a story that might make sense of why they ended up here despite so many people writing it off. And make sense of why I can't stop coming back, years after I thought I left for good.

* * *

Blinded. Stunned. In the still-warm winter days of November 2021, I drove the four hours, give or take,

down to Mobile from my parents' house in Montgomery with a mission in mind. I had signed up for a tour
of Africatown in an air-conditioned minivan driven
by Eric Finley, gregarious tour guide, amateur historian, and fair-skinned son of a Black Mobile family. I
wanted to see the place that had been home to some of
the last unwilling Africans to come to Alabama, the pre-
decessors of the willing ones like my parents and their
friends. The tour group comprised just me and two
men who had grown up in the area and were interested
in business opportunities, as both private and public
interests descended on Africatown. We were a group
of Black Alabamians who had signed up for a lesson
in Black Alabama history we had never gotten. Seems
about right.

There was a lot of attention around Africatown those
days. The *Clotilda*, the ship that had brought the last
Africans to Alabama for enslavement, and the last slave
ship to return to the United States, had been found in
the Mobile River during the early summer days of 2019.
The narrow, eighty-six-foot-long schooner with big pale
sails had been built to move cargo, not people, and was
in a remote bayou. Now a revitalization and redevelop-
ment committee was presiding over proposals to create
tourist attractions around the discovery and draw in
money, as well as revive existing homes and build new
ones. Eric said there was a welcome center in progress in
the Africatown quarter that would be the starting point
of tours to the ship's wreckage out in the river. One of
my fellow tourists tried to pry more information from

him on other business ventures, but Eric evaded the man's questions.

"You're not gonna get me where you want me," he told him, laughing. "Let's have that comprehensive plan so we don't have this going here, that going here, and none of it is toward the ultimate goal of the descendants and their community, which has been dumped on by every injustice, from economic to environmental, that exists."

Books were being written about Africatown and the *Clotilda*, documentaries were being made, articles were being published. The descendants of Africatown's founders and the descendants of the *Clotilda*'s owner, Tim Meaher, were still living in town and were now receiving requests to talk about their nonexistent relationship; Africatown descendants were also being asked to tell their side of the story in one of the most meaningful ways since Zora Neale Hurston interviewed their forefather Oluale Kossola, or Cudjo Lewis. "Cudjo was a mover and shaker, y'all," Eric told our group. Cudjo, who lived until 1935, had a hand in establishing Africatown's cemetery, the first Black school in the city, and a Baptist church. "He wasn't a very educated person, but he knew how to get things done, and he did," Eric said.

Africatown is now a place of crumbling houses and a green so untamed that the grass and bush are retaking abandoned lots and little-trafficked streets. The community's population is in decline, and residents are suffering from poverty and from the environmental devastation caused by the industries that moved next door to them—like asphalt and paper plants that have been shown to release cancer-causing chemicals. It was the Meaher family's real estate company, which held thirty-five million dollars in assets as of 2012, including 22,000 acres of land, that had leased the property to International Paper and Kimberly-Clark for those plants.

Mobile is a city that evokes feelings of pleasure: waterfront streets of antebellum mansions with wrought iron balconies, golf courses, and parks for boating, fishing, and camping. Symbolically, to Alabamians who live outside it, the city is a place of leisure, where you go to sink into its lazier rhythm, nearby beaches, and bars on Dauphin Street, a corner akin to New Orleans' Bourbon Street. I tend to think of Mobile as the junior brother of New Orleans, that haunted crossing for removed Indians going one way and imported Africans going the other. Looking at it now, Mobile might be the only place in Alabama where Africatown could exist, suspended in an imaginative place between who Alabamians are and who they could be.

Before the Civil War, Mobile was known as Cotton City, as Sylviane A. Diouf writes in *Dreams of Africa in Alabama*—a city of white gold for enterprising white men and a way station of despair for enslaved Africans. Mobile was the country's second-largest exporter of cotton after New Orleans. Diouf writes that a journalist recorded after his visit there in the 1850s: "People live in cotton houses and ride in cotton carriages. They buy cotton, they sell cotton, think cotton, eat cotton, drink cotton, and dream cotton. They marry cotton wives, and unto them are born cotton children." Just one thing made the city go around.

As the only major port in Alabama, Mobile was the commercial center of the slave trade: there were sixteen insurance companies that protected bondspeople, boats, and crops; sixteen consulates of foreign countries that imported goods from Alabama; and lots of wealthy planters, merchants, middlemen, and steamship captains who were making it rich on the wild Gulf Coast.

As our tour group meandered through the city, we each reminisced about going to Mardi Gras in Mobile back in our childhoods, catching Moon Pies thrown from floats; one guy remembered a time when tiny bottles of liquor were thrown. Eric said he had to tell us about an enslaved man near the border with Mississippi named Wallace Turnage, who ran away from his plantation four times and got caught going north every try. Turnage was born in North Carolina, the son of an enslaved girl and a white man; his life as a slave took him unwillingly through the South. One of his masters ended up selling him in Mobile—we drove right past a former slave market on Royal Street—to a local merchant who had a home near the current Saenger Theatre. Eric pronounced the word *theatre* the way people do around these parts, with three stretched-out syllables starting with "thee" and then resting on a flat *a*, like the one in "ate."

There weren't a lot of plantations in Mobile back in Turnage's time; it was a seaport town. During the Civil War, he was driving the merchant's carriage on Dauphin Street when a harness broke, flipping it over. The merchant viciously beat him. So Turnage fled once again, in this instance heading south. "He wasn't taking another beating. He ran out the door, and he ran south. And if you run south around here, you know you gonna run in the water," Eric told us. We laughed.

Turnage crossed swamps and rivers to reach the city's southern tip, where he hid in a ditch from Confederate soldiers. One day, he saw Union troops at a fort across the waters of Mobile Bay. "He couldn't figure out how to get over," Eric went on. But Turnage found a rowboat the size of a bathtub and headed toward the Union soldiers' camp. Before he got there, a Union boat scooped him up. The soldiers told him they could help him escape, the story went, if he told them everything he knew. If not, he could go on back to his master's house. Turnage, who wrote a memoir narrative that was published almost a century after his death, told them what he knew. He would reunite in North Carolina with his mother and siblings, whom he hadn't seen in years, and end up in New York a free man.

On the last stretch of our tour, we wound through the historically Black area of Mobile and down a street that Eric called "the Black Main Street," where Black businesses once stood. We paid respect to the spots where a Black-owned drugstore, part of a local chain, had operated, and to other places: law and newspaper and dentist's and accountant's offices. Most of the businesses had invested in a Black-owned bank, which got going partly because the white bank didn't want to hire Black tellers or loan money to Black people, Eric said. The community opened Black-owned clothing and grocery stores because the white ones didn't want to hire black sales clerks in the 1950s and '60s.

Civil rights marches had come down the street. An alternate town, an alternate story, until the city eventually cleared the neighborhood. "They blindsided the community with urban renewal. I call it urban *removal*," Eric said. "They said, 'We gotta clean up the avenue.' That this is the ghetto. They took all of these businessmen out of the market, and demolished our cohesiveness as a race here." The paper mills did a similar thing to Africatown. The other two men on the tour nodded and said, "Mmhmm, that's right." Nearby, we saw the first African American mortuary in the city. There was one more stop, a Black church that boasted the oldest Baptist congregation in the state. The story goes that a slave owner freed a group of his enslaved people because they worshipped so feverishly it gave him headaches and nightmares. In 1806, those newly free people founded the congregation of what would become Stone Street Baptist Church. Survivors of the *Clotilda* and their families later joined the church.

The congregation of Stone Street Baptist came together thirteen years before Alabama was a state. It had been here with the Creek and the white settlers and everyone else who had found themselves in this wild territory. Statehood would control much of that wildness, solidify power in the inheritance of some and guarantee that the rest of us would keep fighting for it along the way. Those fights were visible for all to see—from the actual wars, to the activism, to the allegiance to family, to the seizure of independence through business empire, to the refusal to leave, to the decision to come back.

By the time I was in elementary school, my sense of connection to other West Africans in Alabama was weaker than that of my parents and, before them, of the founders of Africatown. My mom had come to appreciate having other Nigerians on campus, but she had been wary of them before coming to Alabama State. Because of their country's divisive, corrupt leadership, Nigerians could be distrustful of one another, depending on their ethnic and religious alliances. All I wanted was to be southern and American, in that order. I remember the first time I heard the phrase "African booty-scratcher," something a girl called me in the bathroom—I don't remember if we were fighting or if she was just teasing me. It was the first time I realized other Black kids saw me as different, not really one of them, because of my last name. I never heard the term again, but in high school, a Black friend looked at me in the auditorium one day and told me, with kindness, that while I did resemble our Black classmates, there was something unusual about the way I looked, too—she could tell I was not from here. There were other African kids in town, mostly Nigerians, a few Liberians, some Ghanaians. We knew one another because our parents socialized together, but that didn't usually mean we were friends.

We were all leading double lives. On the weekends, we could see one another at house gatherings and barbecues, or at elaborate festivities for Christmas and Nigeria's Independence Day, or at graduation parties and weddings in flowering backyards and churches. On these occasions, our parents would dress us in traditional Nigerian clothing, the girls' waists cinched in long, narrow skirts and fitted blouses, and the boys in slim trousers under too-big tunics. Particularly for the Christmas throw-down, held in a hotel banquet hall, my family and our friends would wear our finest, a sea of blinding-bright textures and elaborate geles that stretched skyward. My mom still has shelves high up in a closet reserved for these times, stacks of stiff embroidered fabric in a spectrum of shades and cuts that nearly hit the ceiling; she pulls up a chair and brings down options from which my brothers and I can choose. At the parties, we'd pile our plates with jollof rice and plantain and pounded yam and stew, as our parents danced to the DJ and caught up with their friends. Once the school week restarted, we were back in jeans and in line for French fries and boxes of chocolate milk in the cafeteria. We acknowledged one another with nods and quick smiles in the hallways; otherwise, we moved in different spheres.

There was little need to lean on one another as our parents had when they were students, because the Americanization process was almost complete: aside from our foreign names, we were Black Americans, born and raised in this country, generally unfamiliar with our parents' homelands and desperate to be seen as part of this one. If only we had known that we were no newcomers, that people like us had been among the first, too: from 1870 to 1880 in Alabama, as Diouf records, at least a thousand people reported having African parents. We had done nearly everything our parents wanted, yet were quickly becoming people they hadn't expected. We got mostly good grades, participated in the right intellectual activities, but we often thought differently about the people we wanted to be and the futures we wanted to have.

Sometimes, our thoughts coincided. During those Nigerian parties, as Fela Kuti and King Sunny Ade played from the speakers, I would inevitably end up staring at my mother's girlfriends, married or divorced or single women, as they floated around the hall eating, talking, laughing. Their hair and makeup were exquisitely done, with big curls and updos, red lipstick and vivid eye shadow; their outfits, planned weeks in advance, melded glamour and comfort, so they could sweep you up into their folds of crinkly, glittering fabric as they danced; and their jewelry, usually gold or coral, was dramatic. Their shoes and purses always matched. The ease they had in their bodies, no matter what they looked like, was astonishing. *Move out of the way, or we'll move over you. Enjoy what you're seeing, or close your eyes.* Their swagger seemed both over-the-top and effortless.

I was never sure how exactly to define my relationship to those women in my parents' life. My parents' sisters were naturally my aunts, beloved by my brothers and me. But their friends, especially my mom's, were also a constant part of the background, in our home, in their homes, and at important moments like birthdays—as reliable a presence as my aunts, though they weren't relatives. My mom instructed me to refer to all of them as "Auntie," anyway. The women existed in an unusual space. They were not my "age-mate," as Nigerians like to say, not people I could treat like my school and neighborhood peers. But over time, they became like family. They flooded me with love and praise, but also disciplined me, shouting my name as a warning when I got out of line or ran around like a heathen. (In fact, sometimes I wanted to shout back that they were not my mom.)

Along with my mom, my aunties presented visions of what life could look like when I eventually decided who I would be—a panorama of Black womanhood that included professionals and entrepreneurs, stay-at-home mothers, perpetual students getting degree after degree, and those who went among all those statuses. One, betrothed when she was young and living in Nigeria and eager to start a life in America, came to Alabama to be with her husband, a man in our community; she became a shop owner and a respected figure in town. Another was a doctor equally as ambitious as her doctor husband; later in life, she became obsessed with marathons, running them all over the world.

My aunties' general passive aggressiveness about what I was doing with my life—was I still planning to go to law school, when would I get married and have children, what exactly was I wearing that day—was also part of my young adulthood. Nigerians are nothing if not obsessed with status, trying to project high status, and obsessing over what others think of their status. But it comes with love.

The lack of distinction between my "real" aunts and my aunties was even more acute when my family visited Nigeria when I was in the sixth grade. There, every girl older than me in our social circles took it upon herself to act as my surrogate mother. Aunties have a singular role: whether or not they have children, they are maternal figures to the young people around them—a phone call away with guidance, able to step in if parents are overwhelmed with work or personal crises. In Nigeria and across the African continent, as people grow older they gain more admiration for their experience and wisdom, unlike in the States, with its obsession with youth. When I was a child, my parents made sure I always greeted the older people in the room appropriately. It is rarely heard of to put aging relatives in senior homes; instead, they often move in with their children until they pass on.

So, older aunties were figures of authority; they helped make decisions for our local association of African families. I remembered one of my aunties emceeing our annual holiday party with a mic in one hand and the train of her skirt in the other, roasting all the families, and sitting in my family's living room consoling my parents after one of my grandparents died. Naturally, drama arose among my aunties, and between my parents and my aunties, from disagreements to gossip. But everyone eventually came around. Some of them had been friends since they were at Alabama State. They were all they had.

My aunties and my mom had to will themselves into being in a place that had ostensibly welcomed them, then had no idea what to do with them. Their former Black classmates tolerated them, and their current Black and white colleagues and neighbors treated them with varying levels of friendliness and remove. (Though my parents did have some good Black Alabamian friends, times when the mutual distrust disappeared.)

Other immigrants and newcomers have tended to shrink in response to the indifference or hostility of their adopted homes, tried to blend in, assimilate, disappear. My mom and aunties only grew in size; it was probably genetically impossible to do otherwise. Their clothes were loud, their voices were loud, their approaches to life were loud. They treated their new home like a stage that would have to bend to their directions. It was a resilience necessary for survival. Their extreme West African femininity both clashed and agreed with the archetype of southern white womanhood. My mom desperately wanted me to wear earrings more, do my hair more, put on dresses more; she also wanted me never to bow to anyone.

Inspired by an assignment from *Vogue* magazine, I would come to call the way my aunties presented themselves, their outside-facing attitude and demeanor, "auntie style." My editor had wanted me to write an essay that would go along with a photo story on West African women's fashion; I agreed without knowing what I was going to say. Then I thought about my personal Africatown. I wrote in the essay that auntie style is mostly ephemeral, an unbothered mood, but still tangible: I know it when I see it. Like a middle-aged woman on the street in New York or London, flamboyantly put together and cradling a phone to her ear, as she balances shopping and grocery bags and herds her kids home while speaking Yoruba and English to her caller and her children at the same time. Being an auntie is also physical, manifesting in a volcanic and inebriating presence. I eventually realized that the only kind of womanhood I subscribed to, that I agreed to belong to, was shaped by the Black aunties in my life.

It was in high school that I started to question if belonging was even what I wanted. It seemed more interesting, going by the novels I loved by Madeleine L'Engle and others, to coolly observe what happened in my world instead of losing myself in it. Restraint in favor of excess. I lived in my head so much as a child, imagining other lives, that it became natural to feel I was both part of what was happening, and apart from it, too.

That was how I kept looking at Alabama when I came back to start reporting and writing here. Everything was familiar, but nothing was for certain. When I was growing up, that feeling of apartness was more real to me than a sense of suffering from racism. I argued with classmates who wore Confederate flag T-shirts, but it affected me more that the story of families like mine was that we didn't quite belong. Our real home was somewhere else—the same story my parents were told at Alabama State, the one they told themselves. But the truth is that we have always been here: as the founders of Africatown, as immigrants that have come since then, as inheritors of this bloodied, gloriously fecund land.

For Further Reading

Barracoon: The Story of the Last "Black Cargo," by Zora Neale Hurston.

Bloody Lowndes: Civil Rights and Black Power in Alabama's Black Belt, by Hasan Kwame Jeffries.

Capitol Men: The Epic Story of Reconstruction Through the Lives of the First Black Congressmen, by Philip Dray.

Claiming Tribal Identity: The Five Tribes and the Politics of Federal Acknowledgment, by Mark Edwin Miller.

Corazón de Dixie: Mexicanos in the U.S. South Since 1910, by Julie M. Weise.

Creek Country: The Creek Indians and Their World, by Robbie Franklyn Ethridge.

Dixie's Daughters: The United Daughters of the Confederacy and the Preservation of Confederate Culture, by Karen L. Cox.

Dreams of Africa in Alabama: The Slave Ship Clotilda *and the Story of the Last Africans Brought to America*, by Sylviane A. Diouf.

Dumping in Dixie: Race, Class, and Environmental Quality, by Robert. D. Bullard.

Here We May Rest: Alabama Immigrants in the Age of HB 56, by Silvia Giagnoni.

The Indicted South: Public Criticism, Southern Inferiority, and the Politics of Whiteness, by Angie Maxwell.

Neither Carpetbaggers nor Scalawags: Black Officeholders During the Reconstruction of Alabama, 1867–1878, by Richard Bailey.

The Politics of Massive Resistance, by Francis M. Wilhoit.

Race and Reunion: The Civil War in American Memory, by David W. Blight.

Remembering the Civil War: Reunion and the Limits of Reconciliation, by Caroline E. Janney.

The Rise of the Poarch Band of Creek Indians, by A. Lou Vickery.

South and West: From a Notebook, by Joan Didion.

The Southern Mystique, by Howard Zinn.

They Say the Wind Is Red: The Alabama Choctaw—Lost in Their Own Land, by Jacqueline Anderson Matte.

Acknowledgments

This book would not be here without the warmth, generosity, and wisdom of Jin Auh, Sarah Crichton, Serena Jones, Barbara Jones, David Remnick, Maya Fuhr, Sammy Loren, Sarah Kinosian, Kate Linthicum, Tristan Reed, Nike Lawrence, Anh-Thu Ngo, Maya Levin, Mansi Choksi, J Wortham, Chioma Nnadi, Mennlay Aggrey, Lauren Bohn, Anna Day, Tara Aghdashloo, Tre Borden, Adwoa Adgeyman, Jennifer Rochlin, Nientara Anderson, Dayo Olopade, Nana Mensah, Anais Borja, Lauren Collins, Nicki Sobecki, Sarah Cannon, Ian Blair, Angela Flournoy, Elaine Braithwaite, Leeor Wild, Conor O'Neil, Idil Abshir, Elizabeth Williams, Alex Foster, and Cyrus Dunham. And of my family, as always.

Thank you to Stephanie, Calvin, Mary, Tina, and Brandon for your time and honesty. Thanks to my parents for sharing their stories with me and putting me up with love every time I came home, drove their cars all over the state, and ate much of their food.

Also, much gratitude to the institutions that provided space and resources for the writing of this book: the International Women's Media Foundation, MacDowell, Yaddo, the Robert B. Silvers Foundation, and the Russell Sage Foundation. Appreciation to Hometown Action, Alabama Contemporary Art Center, and my fact-checker Elizabeth Barber-Sloma.

About the Author

Alexis Okeowo has reported on conflict, human rights, and culture across Africa, Mexico, Europe, and the American South for the *New Yorker* and other publications. Okeowo is the author of *A Moonless, Starless Sky: Ordinary Women and Men Fighting Extremism in Africa*, which received the 2018 PEN Open Book Award. Her work has also been anthologized in *The Best American Sports Writing* and *The Best American Travel Writing*. Okeowo was named journalist of the year by the Newswomen's Club of New York in 2020 and received the Phillip D. Reed Environmental Writing Award in 2022.